GW01457997

BLOCKBUSTER

Dean Crawford

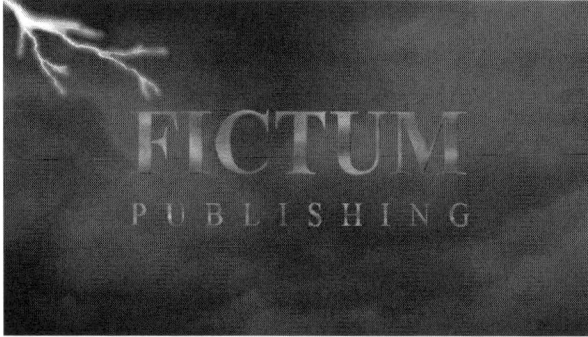

© 2016 Dean Crawford
Published: 13th October 2016
ISBN: 1541087437
ISBN-13: 978-1541087439
Publisher: Fictum Ltd
The right of Dean Crawford to be identified as author of this Work has been
asserted by him in accordance with sections 77 and 78 of the Copyright, Designs
and Patents Act 1988.
All rights reserved.

www.deancrawfordbooks.com

I: Introduction – *Why me?*

There have been countless books published about the art of writing over the years. Many of them are great and filled with hints, tips and tricks to help the aspiring newcomer to the world of writing overcome the many stumbling blocks in their way. So why should you read this one and not the dozens, perhaps hundreds of others available?

Well, I have a major advantage in that few of the other self–help books are written by genuinely bestselling authors. That of course does not mean that they're insufficient for your needs, but it does beg the question of how much those authors can truly know about crafting a novel that has *the chance* of becoming a true high–flier? Some of them are written by authors or editors who proudly proclaim to be *Amazon #1 Bestsellers!* Cursory investigation often reveals them to have reached the *#1* position in an obscure Amazon sub–category, their true overall rank nothing like bestselling. This has become probably the most abused claim to publishing success: Twitter alone is filled with so many supposed *Amazon #1 Bestseller* authors that it's a wonder they haven't all long since retired to the Bahamas to bask in their fame and fortune. Their books will tell you that if you just read them, *you'll* make it. *You'll* be a bestseller too. *Honest* you will…

I am not one of those authors. I've sold hundreds of thousands of copies of my novels, hit the *Sunday Times* bestseller lists with titles distributed by publishing giants *Simon & Schuster* and *Touchstone Books*, and reached not just Amazon's Top #100 Paid with my independent titles but the Top #20 Paid: the front page of *all* of Amazon's books.

I began writing in 1995 with an aim to becoming a published and professional author. In September 2010, I signed my first book deal with a major publisher for a tremendous advance payment and my life changed forever. Sounds great, no? But look again at those dates: 1995 – 2010. It took me *fifteen years* of solid, continuous effort to go from zero to hero. In all those years I never earned a single penny from my writing and I collected over one hundred rejection letters from literary agencies before I finally struck gold.

Fifteen years. That is often the reality of trying to break into a career in publishing. Many try, few succeed, and the few who do succeed rarely earn the kind of advance deals that I did. If that sounds like odds you'd rather not challenge then you may as well close these pages.

No matter how successful an author may or may not become, writing is a *job*, make no mistake. However, it's also a rather wonderful job if you're passionate about the written word and about thrilling your audience, and therefore a full–time occupation as an author really can feel like a dream come true. This book won't spout crap about how you'll make billions in revenue and be the next, great super–star of commercial fiction. So, what *can* it do?

In short, this book is designed specifically to save you as much as possible of those fifteen years it took me to perfect my method of writing, and give your book the *best possible chance* of success. This book cannot guarantee you a globally genre–shattering hit of epic proportions because *nothing* can – if you're looking at buying into somebody else's self–help writing book because it promises anything like that, then drop it like a ticking bomb and run like hell. The world's biggest publishers would love to have that kind of confidence in any one title or series, but it rarely happens: big–hitting books most often come out of nowhere. *Fifty Shades of Grey* was self–published before it grew into a world–wide phenomenon; *Harry Potter and the Philosopher's Stone* was sold in the UK for a paltry advance after a year of effort by J. K. Rowling's literary agent, and only later "broke out" in the United States to become a huge success story and change the life of its author. *Gone Girl* was Gillian Flynn's third novel, not her first. Dan Brown was relatively unknown internationally until his fourth novel, *The Da Vinci Code*, struck a chord with readers across the globe. Lee Child's *Jack Reacher* series took several years to "suddenly" break out and secure its author's fame, fortune and future.

No debut author in the world can write a guaranteed bestseller because they haven't yet got a string of hits behind them or built the kind of audience required to create such a hit. What a new author *can* do is write a book that is good enough that the majority of the obstacles to success are removed, and that's the process that takes so much time. I wish that I had been able to find a good book on the craft of writing way back in 1995 when I first started out, but the compulsion to just get on and *write something* was too strong for me. If you share that compulsion – if you simply *cannot* stop yourself from writing, then this is the book for you. Its contents are built around the methods that I use to craft my novels, honed and perfected over many years of hard graft. Those rules and skills apply to all genres, because so much of what we do as authors is centred around getting those readers to keep *turning those damned pages!*

Whatever else happens, however else we may differ in our approaches, our styles and our genres, keeping the reader engaged both within the story and, a crucial aspect often ignored by authors, *after* the story has ended, is a skill that must be mastered. If any author is going to have a chance of competing with a world of other talented writers all struggling for a place in the market, they must learn to write fiction that is compelling enough for readers to just keep turning those pages.

If you think that you're up for it, that you're an author who can't *not* write, then over the following pages I'll take you every step of the way as you work on your own masterpiece and beyond, because this book isn't just about writing a novel. This book won't just cover your planning, plotting, character development and editing. It will detail the submission process to literary agents, your approach to publishing houses, and if you're intending to go it alone as an independent author (seen by many as the smarter route these days) the means and skills required to produce your cover artwork, editing, proofing and marketing and how to launch your book to a new audience.

In addition, this book will be regularly updated to keep pace with the ever–changing world of publishing, with links to contributors and useful websites at the end of the book updated to keep everything as current as possible. The date of the latest update will appear at the end of this introduction.

So, it's all down to you. You can close these pages and go buy that other self–help book that promises you the world if you want. Or you can follow the advice of a *genuine* bestseller who has earned well over one million dollars from my writing since 2010, who has seen both sides of the publishing world and developed the skills to produce full–length novels single–handed. Go take one more look at the other books available, and then make your decision.

It's your call…

Latest update: December 2016

May, 1993

I can remember the first time I realized I could become a writer. Two years previously I had learned at the ripe old age of eighteen that my lifelong dream of becoming a fighter pilot would never happen. A recent eye–test had revealed that I was slightly color blind, meaning that I could never serve either as a military or commercial pilot.

For somebody who had held that dream since the age of eight it was a tough blow to take. I dealt with it as any mature and sensible teenager would, by sulking for about a year. The fact that I lived next to a military airbase where many of our family friends were fighter pilots didn't help much. Watching them rocket off into the blue five days a week was difficult to say the least, knowing that I would never be able to join them.

Despite everything, over time I decided to pick myself up and sought another life goal. A few months spent training with airborne infantry in the Territorial Army convinced me that soldiering wasn't a future for me, but then inspiration came from an unexpected source. My uncle, Christopher Jarvis, had recently gone full–time as an artist in oils, acrylic and water color and was thoroughly enjoying his life. I wondered if there was something similar that I could do; a job that I might love rather than one that just paid the bills. I was sitting reading a Wilbur Smith book one day when I was struck by a sudden thought – I could write a novel!

I was genuinely surprised that I hadn't thought of it before. I'd always loved creative writing in school. At about the same time I read a newspaper article detailing the dramatic rise to success of a British thriller author, Michael Ridpath, whose debut "Free to Trade" was soaring up the charts and had made him some serious money. The stereotypical image in my mind of an author being an impoverished old guy rattling a typewriter in a dusty attic vanished: this was a career move, something worthwhile that could earn me a living.

All I needed to do was pen a blockbuster…

PART 1: THE CRAFT OF WRITING

The first part of this book will deal with the art of writing your first novel. It is possible of course that you're already well–versed in writing techniques, perhaps having already got a couple of books under your belt. However, if those titles have yet to sell then you might find the next few chapters useful in dissecting what in your writing works and what doesn't work.

We will cover plotting, planning, '*pantsing*' and structure. I'll help you consider dialogue, character, the conventions of creative writing and share as many of my writing tips and exercises as I can to help you get started. Then we'll move into pace, mystery, conflict and tension. Finally, I'll help guide you through the often–arduous task of editing your novel so that it becomes as good as it can possibly be.

Part Two of this book will deal with what happens *after* you've finished your novel. This is an often–neglected part of most self–help creative writing books, largely because so few authors have trodden the rocky roads of both traditional publishing and independent publishing. I'll show with examples how best to approach literary agents, what to expect from them, what contracts you might be offered by publishers and how much you might get paid. We'll cover royalties, foreign sales and other details of the process.

Finally, I'll talk about independent publishing and show you how to go it alone if your book can't find a home with a publisher, or if you're an enterprising spirit and want full control of your writing destiny.

Welcome to the world of writing books…

II: I don't know where to start…?

Not me, you.

It's probably the most oft–quoted line in the history of people *not* writing books; *I wouldn't know where to start.* Although it may not apply to you if you've already got a tremendous idea for a novel just bursting to get out, I'm willing to bet that many of you will be struggling with this dilemma. What should I do first? Just start writing? Start planning? Start creating characters?

In short, none of the above.

The first step to getting your career off to a good start is figuring out not what you should write, but what *genre* you should be writing in. It sounds obvious but one of the biggest mistakes new writers make is to look at the BIG names in writing, see what they're doing and try to emulate them in order to make their fortune. Publishers and literary agents' slush piles are permanently awash with clones of the latest bestsellers, but what the authors who created these endless tides of sycophantic verse don't realize is that by the time a novel becomes a "break out" hit, it's often already too late to follow it up with something similar. The reason for this is the publishing schedules of the major houses: if they buy a title, it can be up to two years before that novel hits the bookshelves of your local shop, by which time the new fad has run its course and publishers are already looking for something new. I can't bring myself to imagine what depths of literary depravity industry professionals had to wade through in the wake of the success of *Fifty Shades of Gray*.

Don't try to copy anybody else. With luck, you'll have been inspired to write as a result of reading your favourite author – I know I was. In 1995 I'd been reading a lot of Wilbur Smith, who has carved a tremendous bestselling career out of historical novels based in South Africa for many decades now. Wilbur writes terrific action adventure and has sold hundreds of millions of copies, and that's what I decided that *I* wanted to do in order to make my fortune: I was going to be the *next* Wilbur Smith. After four years spent writing three high–adventure historical novels filled with everything from pirates to Napoleonic armies, I realized that I actually wanted to write modern thrillers because that's what came most naturally to me. The problem wasn't that I couldn't write good action and historical adventure, it was simply that I was trying to be the next Somebody Else and not the first Me. So, save yourself a few years right away and don't try to be Wilbur, James Patterson, Gillian Flynn or anybody else but yourself.

I would recommend looking at your own bookshelves and thinking for a while on what you get most excited about reading. You may be loving one author's work right now, but is it a genre that you'd feel comfortable writing in yourself? I didn't feel confident about writing a straight crime novel until nearly twenty years after I first started writing – they all seemed so complex and detailed! How could I achieve success against such talented competition? Was it wise to invest months in a project that might not work out in the end? How could I come up with something genuinely new in such a crowded genre?

This first step, if well thought out, will put you on the right course from the get go.

Think about the kind of books that grab your attention in your local bookstore, the ones that you lay eyes on and think: *"Wow, I've just gotta buy that right now or my life will never again be complete!"* Those ideas that excite you the most, with the blurbs on the back jacket that promise so much and compel you to part with your money in order to find out what's going to happen in the story. These are the kinds of books you most likely will enjoy writing the most. It doesn't matter which genre it is, all that matters is it's the one for you.

It's perhaps worth thinking about subtly crossing genres, although one has to be careful about this. For instance, if your passion is for cozy mysteries or perhaps horror, then you've got something of a problem in terms of how large the market is for your work. The biggest markets are in romance, crime and thrillers, generally in that order. Things like mysteries, horror and science fiction come somewhat further down the line. Don't let that deter you, however – I also write science fiction alongside my thrillers and there's always a readership for them. It's just a little harder to find than if you're aiming at the largest markets where it's easier to create a real hit down to simple demographics: more readers, more sales.

As a result, a cozy mystery author might think about including some level of romance in their novel; or perhaps a science fiction author might ensure a healthy dose of action and perhaps thriller elements to ensure a broader appeal. In essence that's what commercial fiction is – the ability to appeal to as broad an audience as possible and thus garner the best possible sales for your work. It's also the reason that most literary fiction – the "purple–prose" books, don't sell much in comparison. The majority of the reading public can't be bothered with authors who like to spend three chapters describing the contents of an empty box.

So, find what you love to read and can't stop thinking about writing for yourself and you're already well on your way to beginning your career. Now comes a tricky bit, if you're not already a voracious reader (*why not?!*). Before you put pen to paper, find ten of the most successful books in your newly chosen genre and read them all. That's right, I've completely contradicted myself, right? I said not to copy what others have done…

It's not about copying. There are things called genre "tropes", which in essence means that fans of a particular genre *expect* to see certain things. So in the science fiction "*space opera*" genre, which is plot and character led while largely ignoring technological details (think *Star Wars, Star Trek, Battlestar Galactica* etc) fans will expect to see big space battles, vividly drawn heroes and villains, strange new worlds and cliff–hanging suspense – a really entertaining world. Conversely, fans of "*hard*" science fiction will want to see technology explained in detail, complex world–building, massive back story and intricate political structure along with a study of the implications of all the above – a totally believable and thought provoking world.

Don't skip this step unless you've recently read at least a half dozen books in your genre. It really will save you time if these books are fresh in your mind and you can clearly recall them for the purpose of your first "writing exercise".

EXERCISE 1

As entertainers, which is what we authors are (just like rock stars and *Hollywood* actors but without the drugs and the tantrums) we have to ensure that we give our readers *what they want*. Failure to do so will lose you those readers, so therefore it's good practice to immerse yourself entirely in the kind of worlds that you're hoping to create for yourself. Read, read, read and then read some more. After you've read each book in your chosen genre, sit down and make a note of the following;

• What were the *best* scenes in the book?
• What were the *worst*, or what scenes dragged or forced you to *skim*? Why?
• What things were *similar* to other books that you've read in the genre, and what things were *different*?
• What were the specific *genre tropes* that all of the books *shared*?
• How *long* was each book?
• Did you notice after reading that some books were *longer* than others, or did some flow so well that they *seemed* to actually be shorter novels (an important point to note for later).

Take a look at those novels and the notes you've made and just get a feel for how the authors might have put them together. Sometimes, especially when reading very long or complex novels (anything by Tom Clancy or George R.R. Martin for example) it can seem an impossible task for anybody to have crafted such a fabulously complex and twisting tale. The truth however is that most novels, even the really labyrinthine ones, are actually constructed of a few critical set–pieces that are then stretched out and twisted around by the author to create wonderful tales that are far more complex than their essential parts would at first suggest.

This method of structuring work comes at an early stage in the process of writing but it is never set in stone. Fresh ideas come along, often (irritatingly) half way through the first draft. However, these ideas can change the direction of a novel overnight and are often a blessing in disguise, creating a previously unconsidered twist in the tale or turning a protagonist's best friend into an enemy and villain. Such is the fun of writing a novel and in many ways it's as exciting as reading one – the difference is that you're playing God and you can tease the reader in any way you want, throwing in red herrings and unexpected events that will keep them on their toes and turning those pages.

Once you've immersed yourself in your chosen genre, do you feel confident that you have a good sense of how the books that you've read shared a common theme and "feel"? Are you ready to attempt to create with an entirely new set of characters and plots in your own novel based on what you have learned? If so, it's time to get the pen and paper out.

Pen? *Paper*? Is this guy living in the 19th Century?

No. There are all sorts of programs out there such as *Scrivener* to help plot and plan novels but I don't use any of them. I have a pen, an A4 pad and a simple ring–binder. I also do a lot of pacing, thinking, mumbling to myself and go for long walks to help me think. Besides, actually writing the novel requires a lot of sitting down at a desk and the less time I can spend doing that, the better. If you prefer to use software to plan your novels then go for it, because writing isn't a one–size–fits–all process and you should take advantage of anything that makes things easier or works better for you. However, this is a book about how *I* do it, so as promised I'll show you my method and then you can adapt that process to better suit yourself and your preferences.

While we're on the subject of notebooks, go out and buy one right now! It should be a pocket–sized notebook, and make sure you have a pen to go with it. The reason for this is that ideas can strike out of nowhere and trust me, no matter how certain you are that you'll remember your great idea tomorrow, you won't.

Write things down, all the time. Ideas, snippets of conversation, a great line or pun that a friend cracks. Your friends might wonder if you've gone slightly insane, but those little gems will find their way into a novel of yours in the future and you'll be glad that you wrote them down when you did. You're a professional now, not just a *wannabee*, so start acting like one and get that notebook before you get hooked on the next chapter.

Writing in series

There can be little doubt that writing in series is one of the best ways to build a following. There is a reason that TV dramas, movie franchises and popular novel series tend to succeed more, and for longer, than stand–alone movies, books and television programs. Readers build a relationship with the characters, yearning to see them again when they finish the last pages of a novel, and that is something that is essential to understand as you embark on your new novel.

Can it be the first in a series, or perhaps a trilogy? If the first book is a hit, you're going to want to satisfy your fans with more of the same, furthering the adventures of your protagonists as their story continues. It's also worth mentioning that publishing houses, if they decide that they like your work and want to make an offer for your books, will also be interested in the series potential of anything that you write. One–book–wonders are something that publishers tend to avoid unless they're absolutely stellar and they'll request ideas for your next book before offering for your first, so even at this early stage you will need to consider where you're going after you type "The End".

Spend some time making notes for what could follow this first book of yours. Is it the kind of story that simply *has* to finish at the end of book one, or can your protagonists move on into a new adventure in a sequel novel? You don't need to write in great detail about this yet, and as you develop your plot and characters they will likely define how far you can take things. Just keep it in mind for future reference as you embark on this journey: series books sell better than standalones almost every time.

"The best marketing for my fiction has been to write books in a compelling series in a popular genre, where readers want to hear more about the characters over time. This maximizes your revenue per reader as even if they discover your books later in the series, they will often buy the backlist. Series also enable you to package your books into box–sets, which provide another level of income and are easier to merchandise at Kobo and iBooks, whose customers value higher price books."

J.F.Penn. *New York Times* & *USA Today* bestselling author.

III: Hook, Line and Sinker

Have you ever heard the opening bars of a great song on the radio for the first time and felt the hairs go up on the back of your neck? Even though you'd never heard that track before, somehow you knew it was going to be a belter before the singer even opened their mouth.

Congratulations, you were caught on the end of a "hook".

Hooks come in many forms, and the first hook you'll need to think about when you're sitting down to write a novel is not just what the story is going to be about, but what the story "hook" is. In *Hollywood* parlance, a hook is often referred to as a *high–concept* idea. High–concept merely describes an idea for a story that grabs people instinctively, is highly commercial and especially if it's both of the above and entirely original.

We writers need at the start of a new project to know what our book is going to be about. That might sound obvious but without having a sense of the central theme and point of our story, we don't really have a story at all. The first idea, that central spark of inspiration can be provoked by more than just sitting around trying to think of something to write about, and the hook is often the best way to get the ball rolling.

The hook is in many ways integral to the idea that you're hoping to come up with for your first novel, and it's one of the reasons that I recommend having a notebook with you at all times (or recording / writing something on your cell phone instead if you have a great idea when on the move). All stories have a central concept, something that drives the story forward toward its inevitable climax and provides the backbone of your novel. The hook can sometimes be condensed into a single line of text or thought that encapsulates the essence of your story idea, which can be a useful way to get started with the central concept of your story.

Strong hooks are often the hardest thing to come up with, but wildly exciting when they burst into life inside your mind. Ideas seem to follow them one after the other in an unstoppable flow, and stories can literally be built in hours as a result. One such moment occurred to me in the late summer of 2013, when I began considering whether technology had advanced enough that data storage might conceivably be able to transcribe a living brain into digital form, thus allowing a human being to survive after death. Combined with advances in holographic technology, I conceived of a new species of human: *Holo Sapiens*.

The idea and that unusual, compelling species name sparked a burst of creativity that lasted for hours. I paced up and down our garden under the summer sun and wrote copious notes, ideas, insights and even a single line which neatly encapsulated the entire novel before I'd even written it – the hook;

Mankind is doomed, but death is no longer the end. Which side of the afterlife would you choose?

And so my techno–thriller *"After Life"* was born, and has since sold countless copies as an independent novel. Does reading that line sound like something you might see on a movie poster? Those grab–lines beloved of *Hollywood* are all hooks, designed to give the potential viewer an instant idea of what the book or movie contains, a sense of what they can expect.

Here's another hook / grab–line: see if you can guess where it's from;

An adventure sixty–five million years in the making.

Unless you've been living under a rock in Patagonia for the last three decades there's a good chance you identified it as the hook from the movie *Jurassic Park*, which was itself a bestselling novel by the late Michael Crichton before Steven Spielberg bought the movie option and directed the iconic film.

So how can you achieve something like this, a hook that really fires the imagination? Well, for me it's usually down to inspiration born of something I've seen, heard or read about that fires my imagination. I often get sudden "what if" thoughts about new novels when reading articles in magazines or watching dramas on television. Creativity breeds creativity, and you should begin to think of it as the fuel to your writing aspirations: look *everywhere* for ideas. Read newspapers, surf the Internet, listen to stories told by other people and look out for opportunities in everything that you see. I personally can hardly go a day without having to grab my notebook or even a scrap of paper because something I've seen has provoked a sudden idea in my head. I literally wrote one down about an hour ago on the back of a sheet of paper I was using to make notes about this very chapter. It's something of a wonder to me that everybody isn't having these kinds of *"eureka"* moments every day, but I suppose that's the reason that not everybody is a writer.

"I write for a living, so every time the bank manager gives me an appraising glance I know that it's time to get back to the computer and get stuck in again. The other old expression is that I can only write when the muse is upon me, and I make damn sure that it is upon me at eight o'clock every morning. I've been blessed – or cursed, depending on your point of view – with a work ethic that makes me feel guilty if I'm not writing, so I do tend to spend most of every day sitting in front of the laptop and getting something – anything – written. I've also found that simply asking the question 'What if' about any event in history very often leads me down

interesting and largely unexplored pathways. As a writer it is essential to write, but even more essential to read. Whenever I have a new project in mind, I will spend weeks, sometimes months, digging around on the Internet ▮▮▮▮▮▮▮ *trying to tease out all the information I can that will* ▮ *writing some kind of factual basis and an authenticity tha* ▮ *can never do."*

Peter Stuart Smith, *New York Times* bestselling author

In 2014 I read about a truly remarkable piece of technology created in Japan. A simple brainwave device measured people's responses to being shown images of objects; trees, lakes, aeroplanes, people etc. Computers recorded tens of thousands of these brainwaves, each as unique as a fingerprint. Then, they started asking new subjects to *think* about trees, aeroplanes, people etc while wired to the same device. This time, a computer in another room attempted to match their brainwaves to its data banks of existing brainwaves and thus, to images.

What happened was truly frightening: on the computer screen in the other room, researchers were literally able to *see* what the subjects were thinking about. A perfect, if slightly blurred image of their thoughts appeared on the screen, the resolution of that image sufficient for the researchers to easily identify certain objects (one was a student who was asked to think about the Sydney Opera House). Human thoughts had been translated into visual images on a screen, a remarkable achievement and one that got my own brain racing like an out–of–control freight train. Months later my novel *The Identity Mine* was published, the third in my *Warner & Lopez* series, and was an instant commercial and critical hit largely due to its hook:

Our enemies are no longer hacking ▮▮▮▮▮▮ *Now, they're hacking us…*

Make an effort to search for a fresh angle that will make your novel something more than just another detective series / romance / adventure or whatever your chosen genre is. What will make it *special*? What will make it stand out sufficiently in your own imagination, never mind anybody else's, so that you'll have sufficient enthusiasm and excitement to see the project right through to the end. A hook, and the good idea behind it, is the fuel for your imagination throughout the process and in many respects the ace up your sleeve. Here's another, from author Adam Croft's *Her Last Tomorrow*:

It's every parent's worst nightmare: Nick Connor's five–year–old daughter has been kidnapped. He can have her back on one condition: he must first murder his wife.

Intrigued? Interested? Suddenly compelled to find out what happens? You've been hooked. It's another reason to have read widely in your chosen genre, as many very successful books have capitalised on their author's inspired ideas in order to become so commercially successful. Grab–lines like the one above serve a very useful purpose in our modern age, when people are too busy it seems to spend much time on any one thing. They convey what the reader's going to get in the space of a few short seconds, and can mean the difference between them buying your novel or moving on.

From a writing perspective, they also provide the anchor upon which the story is built. I find that it helps enormously to have that central hook in place fairly early on to guide me as I begin building a story around that one central idea, and if it happens to be something that's based on real world events that's even better. As with *The Identity Mine*, there's nothing quite like making the reader think that the author's imagination has created some mythical, wildly exotic technology, and then quoting from real–world publications and revealing that in fact the technology actually exists, *today*.

Spend some time thinking about how you can take perhaps the first seeds of an idea and apply some new twist to it to make it special. You'll know when it happens because you'll have the same tingle down your spine that you get when you see another author's work with a great hook, or a movie advert that looks awesome and demands to be seen on the big screen. Write them down the moment you get them, even if it's 3am and you don't want to get out of bed (definitely get out of bed because you *won't* remember them in the morning!) because they don't come along every day but when they do they're worth their weight in gold.

So, that's your first step – find that hook. (Cue sound of reader screaming). Yes, I know it's not an easy step and ideas don't just drop out of the sky every morning but you want to be a writer, correct? That means writing more than one book. It may well mean writing dozens of them over the length of what I hope will become a great career. This moment, searching for that great idea, is in many ways both the easiest (it requires only eyes, ears and thought) and the hardest (*I can't think of anything dammit!*).

It will come. The ideas will come. Buy yourself a nice, clean new A4 lined pad and a decent pen and start scribbling. Watch television, especially some of the great dramas and action series being produced in the United States in recent years. Think about plots that you've seen and twist them about to create something new. Watch the news for real–life events and think about whether they might form the basis of something upon which you could build a great story. Take an obvious plot and then turn it on its head, or throw in something completely random and see what sparks fire in your mind. Sooner or later something will click and you'll be on your way.

Believe in yourself, your ideas and your ability, and when you're ready with that great new idea, read on. Because you're going to need somebody through whose eyes the readers will view this new and amazing world of yours. For that, you're going to need some characters.

November 2008

Twelve years.

That was how long I'd been writing. So much for a quick blockbuster! I'd crafted three novels and four screenplays in those twelve years and I had absolutely nothing to show for it. I had just finished my latest novel, "Crossfire", a thriller about the search for a reporter abducted in battle–strewn Afghanistan, and was about to start approaching agents with it when I walked into my local bookstore and almost collapsed.

Former SAS soldier–turned–author Andy McNab had just released his latest thriller; "Crossfire", about the search for a reporter abducted in battle–strewn Afghanistan. I couldn't believe it. Eighteen months of work essentially went down the drain in a split second and my heart sank. Although the internal structure of my novel was significantly different to Andy's (and I later released it on my independent label with a new title, "Revolution") I knew that no literary agent would consider it now.

Deflated, for the first time in twelve years I took some time off from writing. I think I lasted six months before the writing bug took hold again. But this time I decided not to just plunge into another book. I had learned to write but clearly I was behind the curve: other, full–time authors were ahead of me. Somehow, I needed to sit down and come up with an idea so unique that it would stand on its own. It had to be brand new and highly commercial.

I spent a few weeks reading the bestsellers in my own favourite genres, while also watching the bestseller lists and identifying key aspects of what really worked in thriller novels but also what I felt was missing from them. Then, I took my strongest idea for a new novel and began applying all that I had learned from my studies, plotting the new book over a couple of months before starting another year–long slog of writing and editing.

Maybe this one would make it through…

IV: "They're a right character!"

We all know somebody with a strong character, because in essence we're all one in some way or another. The loud mouth. The quiet one. The one who's always laughing. The aggressive one. The friendly one. The nervous one. The weird one (we could all do with less of them). The list is potentially endless…

Your story, no matter what genre it's in or how you choose to tell it, must have fully rounded characters if it's to have the best chance to succeed. The story will unfold through the eyes of your characters so if they are not believable, the story won't be either.

Heroes and villains

Your story will require at least two characters, and those characters must be polar–opposites when it comes to the central goal of your story. Let's suggest, as an example, that you have come up with a compelling story idea about a man who has invented a device that will produce free electricity from thin air.

So, you need a hero to champion this wondrous new device (the hero, or protagonist) and you naturally will also need a villain to oppose him (the antagonist) to create *CONFLICT*.

There, look at that word. Conflict. It's so important I went all *capitally*.

Stories move forward due to conflict, because conflict is an integral part of our need to know what's going to happen next. Having a story where everybody agrees, everybody is aiming for the same goal and where nobody upsets the apple cart is going to be a fairly boring story to read. We will look at conflict in more detail later, but for now it's enough to say that we have a hero and a villain in play.

The free electricity device, known as the *Handybitofkit*, is easy to build and our hero, being a true hero, is not going to sell or patent it. He's going to give it away to humanity. The hero is a good man, with strong convictions that what he has created can change the world for the better. He is suspicious of big corporations and government, and believes in the basic goodness of his fellow human beings.

He believes that wealth resulting from his generosity will come: he just needs a means of achieving it. To that end, he decides to pass the plans for the device to his neighbour for free. If his neighbour builds the device and it works successfully, he pays our hero ten dollars and then passes the plans on again for free with a link to our hero's bank account details. Every person who builds a successful device has saved themselves a lifetime's energy bills, for just ten dollars.

Our hero believes that most people, overjoyed at the savings, will pay him happily. He further believes that the technology will spread so quickly that governments and energy corporations will be unable to stem the tide and a new era of energy freedom will envelop the world with our hero's name at its head.

However, one nefarious recipient of the device decides to sell the information of what's happening to our villain, the CEO of a major local power company. Faced with financial ruin, the CEO must contain the growing crisis and prevent it from spreading to the wider world...

There, with just two characters in play and in the space of just a few paragraphs we have the threads of a great story in place and we haven't even started plotting yet! Now is the time to develop the characters from *your* story before expanding them with further details that will flesh out their depth and make your readers truly believe in their struggle.

Your hero and villain must be at odds with each other, each as determined as the other to reach their goal. Those respective goals must be opposite to each other and the stakes sufficiently high that failure to achieve them could ruin the protagonist or antagonist forever, or even cost them their life.

The hero.

Bottom line, before we do anything else: the reader *must* like the hero. The reader must easily be able to empathise with the hero and they must be rooting for them throughout the whole novel.

As a novice, I used to spend little time thinking about characterization – to a certain extent I'm very fortunate as characters seem to leap fully formed into my mind in a matter of moments and I can just start writing them into the story. However, as I've become more experienced I have realized how important it is to make them as fully rounded as possible, how vital it is for the reader to believe in them. One small slip, one out–of–character action and the reader is jerked out of the story to ask themselves: "Would this character *really* do that? And if they have, is there some *other* reason for it?"

Believe me, there had better be a good reason for a well–established character to do something out of the ordinary, because if there isn't the reader will be disappointed by the end of the book. Don't leave the reader waiting too long for an explanation for why the scrawny, meek librarian suddenly karate–chopped the beefy *Hell's Angel* across the throat without a hint of fear.

Your hero, the story's protagonist, must be at the forefront of all the action and thus must be the most rounded character of all. However, much of that detail should be in the author's mind and portrayed not through description but through character actions and dialogue. The first time your reader meets the protagonist, do not spend four pages detailing every inch of their past in an effort to drill into the reader's brain that they're a reclusive weapons expert who has retreated from military life after a missile accident that killed innocent civilians. Don't regale them with endless paragraphs about his inner pain, his demons, his drinking and his constant struggle to forgive himself, the endless nights and days of grief and loneliness and…

See what I mean? Better to do the following:

Greg awoke to another headache, the lonely winter sunlight scorching his eyes as he hauled himself out of bed and into another day he'd rather not face. Nothing would change. He peered through the cabin's grubby windows out into a frosty wilderness devoid of human company, the nearest town a dozen miles away but not nearly far enough.

There. Not too many words, and yet you're already thinking about Greg as you're reading, right?

Why do this? Because the reader doesn't need to know yet about the missile accident, the deaths and the hero's reclusive grief, and it's best that they shouldn't because in one easy move you've not only described Greg but you've created a *mystery* in the mind of the reader. Why is Greg hungover? Why is he living in a cabin far from civilisation? Why doesn't he want to face another day? Why *why why*?

Mystery is one of the most underrated facets of good, page–turning writing. I don't of course mean mystery in "the butler did it" sense, but the craft of placing questions in the reader's mind even when there's no reason for the reader to suppose the story's actually got going yet. Human beings are innately curious creatures, always questioning things and wanting to know what's behind that closed door, at the end of that lane you've never ventured down, behind those twitching curtains across the street. It's what draws us into a story, our *need to know*. Deny your readers that right to know, stretch it out, make them scream in their mind that they want to know why Greg is apparently depressed and living as a recluse in a cabin in the woods in the middle of winter.

When it comes time to show us Greg's nature, it's best to show it through his actions. So, rather than *tell* the reader that Greg is harbouring great shame and grief, and that it triggers unjust anger that he often takes out on other people, show us. *Show, not tell*. Repeat it to yourself: *show, not tell*. So instead of telling the reader about Greg's anger, show them that anger when he goes to a local store and punches somebody for giving him a dirty look. Why did they give him a dirty look? Why did he hit them without even saying a word? Why do the other townsfolk avoid Greg, whisper among themselves while casting dark glances in his direction, hurry away as he storms back to his truck and drives back off into the wilderness. Why does Greg hit the steering wheel in furious regret at his actions, something that the other townsfolk don't see and is shared only with the reader..?

I just made that all up as I wrote it. Think *fast*, open yourself up to *all* and *any* potential ways of intriguing your audience. Have a mystery of some kind in every chapter if you can manage it (there's more about the use of mystery in fiction later on in the book).

Of course, you *must* engender sympathy and empathy for your hero or your readers are going to find it hard to want to follow their journey. In Greg's case, I've just decided that he tried to stop the missile tests because he felt that the weapons were dangerously unreliable. His superior officers ignored him, the ensuing accident killed a family of four and the military pinned the blame on Greg after his superiors denied they were warned of any flaws in the weapon. Greg is not a bad man; he's been wronged and served ten years in prison as a result, and now he's on the warpath to prove his innocence…

The townsfolk know he's an ex–convict and suspect him of being a murderer or bank robber. They don't like him and don't want him in town. But then at some crucial moment Greg performs an act of great courage – maybe he rescues a child from a burning car, in front of the townsfolk. Attitudes begin to change, questions are asked and the truth starts to come out… That's the bones of a thriller, right there.

Think fast and broad. *Show*, don't *tell*. Believe in your ideas.

Say it like it is.

A good way to flesh out characters is to make a simple list. Some authors advocate drawing up immensely detailed character studies recording every inch of the hero's life prior to the beginning of the story. I don't personally have a problem with this but upon the act of writing a first draft, characters have an alarming tendency to develop as they go along in ways that the author may not have previously considered. This can also be a trait that is hindered if an author over–develops a character before the first draft: the characters can end up having to be shoe–horned into acts that may not suit them and their evolving characters.

I think that it is far better to make some general observations about your characters before a first draft, and go from there. A post–it note with a few brief but revealing lines is all we need. What does Greg look like? How do we imagine he appears? How old is he? How heavy? How does he walk? What leaps into my mind instinctively based on the short passages I wrote earlier in this chapter – see how it compares to your own mental image;

• Greg is in his late thirties, early forties. He's rugged looking, broad shouldered, probably has a beard or heavy stubble and can handle living in the cold and the wilderness.
• He's about two hundred pounds, six foot tall or a bit less, has a sturdy gait, likes wearing lumberjack shirts, thick jackets and probably baseball caps to partially conceal his appearance to avoid recognition.
• He doesn't say much – one word answers or short lines. He avoids eye contact, is terse and has something of a chip on his shoulder. If he does befriend

somebody he becomes warmer but is likely sarcastic, has a dry sense of humour and is hard to really get to know.

Did you come up with something similar? It's quite likely as Greg has some kind of military background as a weapons expert, isn't afraid of living in a remote cabin in a cold climate and has a habit of punching people. Robust, rough and ready is the stereotype Greg fits into.

Some people think that this kind of character stereotyping is a bad thing. I've often been watching a television drama of some kind, where for instance a mad scientist has a nuclear bomb and the good guys are after him, with the hero being the only person capable of stopping the villain from carrying out his evil plan. I can already hear the cries of *"oh as if he would just happen to be in the right place, at the right time and with the right skills to save the day!"*

Well, yes, he would. If terrorists struck at the heart of New York City tomorrow, the government would not deploy a team of highly skilled dentists to hunt them down and kill them, would they? The government would deploy Special Forces units, or elite police armed response teams, the FBI, the CIA and who knows who else. Precisely the kind of people with just the right training and skills to oppose the enemy. While I would agree that there are perhaps a few too many ex–SAS soldiers of fortune cropping up in modern action thrillers these days, it none the less fits the reader's expectations of what kind of character would be called upon in order to save the day. Don't be afraid to put the right character in place as your hero and bless them with the skills that they need to complete the goal you're setting up for them.

The villain.

The same rules apply to the villain as to the hero but most usually the villain's motivations are the mirror–image of the hero's, diametrically opposed to his or her goal. That all important *conflict* comes into play whenever the hero tries to move toward that goal, however it's important to think about the believability of the villain.

It can be tempting to immediately cast them as a cruel, self–centered, callous individual with no interest in or empathy with the rest of the world. However, this instinctive reaction is a bad idea: a villain's motivations and desires must be every bit as strong and believable as those of the hero, even though the reader may not agree with those motivations and will rail against them in their mind.

In the case of our *Handybitofkit* device story described earlier, the villain is the CEO of a major power company. A free energy device would utterly destroy his business empire overnight and so must of course be opposed. The stereotyping in our minds has probably by now created an image of:

• A wealthy, suited man, older, perhaps hawkish and clever.

• Driven by greed and avarice, a modern–day Scrooge who cares little for others

    • A Republican in the USA, or a Conservative if based in the UK

    • Surrounded by lawyers, supported corrupt politicians

    • Possibly the smoker of fat cigars, and maybe overweight himself, bloated by greed

Obviously this villain is determined to protect his business but greed doesn't have to come into it. Being the villain of a story doesn't mean that he has to be any of the above.

What if he has a family who need his financial support? Children, a sick and elderly mother? What if he isn't exactly a villain at all, but imprisoned by the demands of shareholders who will see him removed from his job if he doesn't shut our hero down? This could be a mystery that you hint at early in the story and reveal in full later on, and represents conflict within the antagonist's life that the hero knows nothing about. Conflict must apply to all characters, not just your troubled hero. That combination again is a powerful motivator for plot twists and other storytelling tricks that will keep those pages turning for your readers.

Whatever you decide, and however your story plays out in the battle between your hero and your villain, both characters must be absolutely believable in their motivations and the actions that result from them. Although your antagonist may be a despicable individual, as the author you should absolutely love them! It's incredible fun creating villains, perhaps more so than heroes but at the end of your story your antagonist must be defeated no matter how much you come to like them and their nefarious schemes.

Supporting characters.

Supporting your hero and villain will be a cast of characters, all of whom must also be well thought out and fully–rounded in their character, mannerisms and motivations. Typically, you should keep the numbers of supporting characters down to avoid confusing the reader. Your hero may have one or two faithful companions on their journey, your villain one or two trusted henchmen who share the same goal and motivations.

Normally a supporting cast of characters is only really developed once the plotting and planning for the full story is underway, as this is where they tend to show up as being required in order to move the story forward. We will deal with them here though in order to cover all characters in the same chapter.

This supporting cast should be likewise fleshed out with a clear description of their appearance and well–crafted *show–not–tell* motivations and actions which give readers a vivid portrayal of who they are and what they're like. The characters themselves might not possess quite as much detail as your protagonist and antagonist, but they none the less should be believable and essential to the course of the story.

One of the best examples of characters from movies whom I think portrays best what I mean are the "*minions*" from *Despicable Me,* amusing little yellow creatures with silver goggles and blue denim overalls. They barely spoke a recognisable word, were apparently virtually indestructible and were in many ways minor supporting characters, and yet they were so lovingly crafted in everything that they did that they ended up with their own movie franchise! Think of your supporting cast in this way and take the time to craft them as well as you can.

A further aid to drawing both major and supporting characters is to invest them with certain traits that make them easily identifiable to the reader even though you don't name them on the page. For instance, a male character in your book might walk with the aid of a cane. If that individual has already been portrayed as a prim, well–educated man in his sixties with a superiority complex, then you might be able to introduce them in a later chapter like this:

Marshall heard a rhythmic click of wood on polished tiles from far away down the corridor outside as a voice reached out for him.
'I expect to find you already hard at work, Marshall!'

No name, no direct details of the cane itself – but if the reader has already met the man with the cane in a prior chapter then they'll know who it is all right.

Your novel will require its own set of unique characters, all of whom will need to speak in a different way. It's worth considering also that, in real life, people tend to be attracted to like–minded souls. Groups of friends often get along because to some extent they share the same world views, possess the same values, live in the same streets and such like. In the case of your novel, it's okay for people on the same team to have certain shared goals and similarities – just make sure that one thing above all remains in every chapter, every scene and every page that you write: CONFLICT!

CONFLICT

Yes, it's so important that I went all "capitally" again. It cannot be stated enough: conflict is the driving force between characters in all story telling. Even allies must have conflict: differing opinions, differing tactics and even different motivations from the protagonist's main goal.

Again, there is the notion among novice authors that conflict can only arise in heated moments, such as when a hero is diffusing a nuclear bomb and the sidekick insists that they cut the red wire instead of the blue one. But conflict can take many forms – even subtle, implicit forms where tensions bubble under the surface. Think of occasions when you've heard somebody mutter something sarcastic under their breath, or when glances have been exchanged between two friends over a third–party's foolish comment, and the third party has noticed the exchange but said nothing. *That's* conflict.

The greatest of all human dramas, and the one most effectively utilized in television, is the plot conflict created when two opposing paths collide. Here's a simple one I made up as I was writing this chapter;

The hero absolutely is convinced that the villain will strike their next victim in the city of Boston, but his partner is equally convinced that the villain will strike in Denver. Both are utterly determined to bring the serial–killing villain down, and both are equally obsessed with the glory of doing so. The hero convinces his partner to join him in Boston for a showdown with the evil villain, and that they must work together to achieve an arrest. But before that time comes his partner receives a tip–off that he was right all along – the criminal mastermind is indeed in Denver! But the partner doesn't tell the hero and goes it alone in the hopes of taking all of the glory for himself. The hero arrives in Boston but the showdown doesn't happen and his partner doesn't show, and then he gets a sinister call from the serial–killer He rushes to Denver and finds his partner's mutilated corpse nailed to a crucifix in an abandoned warehouse...

Conflict, in this case leading to tragedy, is a staple of story–telling and its importance cannot be overstated. One of the most common examples in crime fiction is the "maverick" detective and his law–abiding sidekick. The *chalk–and–cheese* relationship stands the test of time by virtue of how often it is utilized by authors and still manages to remain a valid method, and one that entertains seemingly without ever getting clichéd. That relationship expands far further than just crime, however: Luke Skywalker and Han Solo; Foxx Mulder and Dana Scully; Jack Bauer and Chloe O'Brian ; Red Reddington and Elizabeth Keen; Gru and the girls are examples of diametrically opposed characters being forced to work together and the sparks that inevitably fly as a result.

This is what you want *lots* of in your story, the conflict between characters that demands the reader to continue on, to keep turning those pages, so that they can find out what happens next. It's not just for the readers – having such conflict provides fuel for new scenes as you, the author, come up with new ways to put your characters at loggerheads and thus new consequences for the ways in which they deal with their dilemmas.

First person or third person?

A lot of authors struggle with this question, and more than once in my early career I spent many long hours converting an existing manuscript from first person to third person because I just couldn't tell the story while trapped within one character's point of view.

There's a lot of conflicting advice out there, but both methods of story–telling have huge advantages and disadvantages;

1st person: It's possible to create impressive depth of character and the reader literally lives the story through the protagonist's eyes, experiencing their fears, failures and victories as though they were their own. However, the author cannot view the world outside of that character's eyes within the novel, limiting their ability to tell a story with effective breadth.

3rd person: This method allows for tremendous versatility in story–telling with many potential characters at the writer's disposal, all of whom can experience their parts of the story fully. Tension can be easily built between conflicting scenes. However, it becomes harder for the author to manage all points of view and also difficult to differentiate between characters if too many are included. Likewise, the reader can become confused unless it's handled well.

For me, the only real rule is *don't mix perspectives!* Take the time to consider how best your story can be told and then stick with that. Few authors can pull off mixed perspectives and literary agents and publishers will be rightly cautious of a first–time novelist approaching them with such a project. Leave "clever" writing behind until you're already on the best seller lists.

V: Plot is King.

It is sometimes said that there are two kinds of authors and that they can be placed into their own categories: *plotters* and *pantsters*. Plotters, as you may have guessed, like to map out their story before they crack on with the first draft. Pansters on the other hand like to stare at a blank screen for three days while drinking gallons of coffee and agonising endlessly before finally typing their first line. They write by the seat of their *pants*.

I've always plotted my novels but I don't go to the extraordinary lengths that some authors do, in having the entire book outlined to within an inch of its life before they'll even attempt Chapter One. I used to plot deeply, but found that such extremes then caused issues when new and fresh ideas for the storyline leaped into my mind half–way through writing the first draft. Twenty years of experience has told me that the very best method lies somewhere
between *plotting* and *pantsing* and this is how I like to go about preparing to write my first draft. I call this method my Chapter Map.

My Chapter Map typically consists of one to two sides of A4, with a line or two devoted to the events of each chapter in the story. It's intended as a guideline to the first draft, and most usually will change shape during the inevitable redrafts that come later as new ideas come to light during the typing, so it's not like once it's written I can't deviate from it whenever I, or the characters, choose. (Yes, as stated earlier sometimes characters develop lives of their own if you're really getting them down as living, breathing human beings, which you should be).

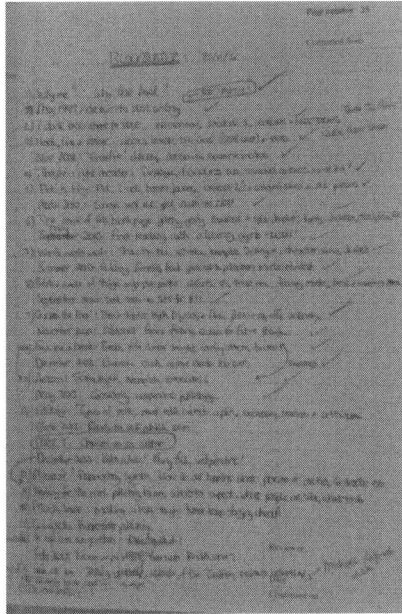

Above is my Chapter Map for this very book (no peeking ahead!).

The fact of the matter is that when it comes to writing, few authors are able to start at page one without a clue of where the story is going and end up with a cohesive manuscript of several hundred pages a few weeks or months later. The only big–selling name I can think of who reputedly does this is Lee Child, author of the successful *Jack Reacher* series, who has claimed that he only ever writes one draft of his novels. I don't doubt that this is true but I wouldn't recommend it, especially if you're aspiring to your first novel. It's not about stifling creativity, which is often the reason most authors defend their *panstering*, but simply about having somewhere for your story to go. If you don't know where the hell your story is going, the chances are that unless you're already a natural story teller with a truly brilliant imagination you're going nowhere fast. If you don't have capacity to control multiple new characters in brand new situations in ways that perfectly fit their completely fresh and undeveloped world, your readers will notice pretty damned quickly.

If you're somebody who naturally prefers to just hit the keyboard and go for it, then don't let me hold you back – hell, it worked out for Lee and Reacher. However, what I'd advise is to at least finish reading this chapter of the book and see if the ideas within help you. Virtually every *pansting* author I've ever known of who had a stab at some basic plotting found that it saved them time later that would have otherwise been wasted procrastinating over their work. It gave them direction in their story, and that's what every story needs. No matter what genre you're writing in, all stories are travelling from the beginning, through the middle and on to the end. If you don't have at the very least that beginning, middle and end in place, your story isn't going anywhere.

Basic Structure

The fundamental basis for all of my novels and upon which I begin all plotting is the Three Act Structure. This method is most commonly used in movie screenplays, and you'll see that it is movies that I will often reference as examples of plotting structure. However, virtually every single novel can be deconstructed to reveal that same act structure, no matter whether the author intended to use it as a plot device or not. The reasons for this are many and a subject for a different kind of book about craft. What's important here is that the three–act structure is one that really works well at keeping the reader engaged within the story while tugging at their anxiety, their sense of escapism, a sense of terrible loss and a sense of victory *in that order*. Of course, the end of many novels is a tragedy and not a victory, but the same structure remains in place and can be broken down simply into the following format;

• *ACT 1*
• The opening, all is normal in our protagonist's world but there may be a hint of trouble ahead. If possible the hook should be right here, ideally on the *first page*.
• The Inciting Event: this is what happens to bring us into the story and shows us a new path that the protagonist must take, often reluctantly.
• *ACT 2*
• The protagonist embarks upon their journey and faces a series of increasingly tough challenges. Allies and villains (the antagonists) make their presence known and either fight for or against the protagonist.
• Through courage and determination the protagonist reaches the centre of the story, the Point of No Return, a crossroads. Either they push on or they abandon their quest, but there can be no turning back from either path.
• The protagonist pushes on against ever greater threats and higher stakes, and almost reaches their goal when…. A great calamity plunges them into despair and loss. They have failed, and there seems to be no hope.
• *ACT 3*
• In deep despair and seemingly defeated, the protagonist finally finds a hint of hope remaining and in a last–ditch attempt to save the day they push on with all that they have left.
• In a final, climatic showdown with the antagonist, the protagonist prevails and defeats their sworn enemy and achieves their goal, often at great sacrifice to themselves.
• **Denouement**: the last plot lines are tied up and the protagonist goes forward, their character changed by their experiences.

Building upon this basic structure is "The Hero's Journey", which follows the same basic format but also includes further conventions such as the "Inexperienced Youth", the "Trusty Sidekick", the "Wise Elder", "The Noble Goal" and so on. Outlined by Joseph Campbell, the hero's journey has become the basis for many of the most successful stories of modern times in both film and television. George Lucas relied heavily upon it when he wrote the screenplay *Star Wars*, should you need any convincing of its power in structured story telling. In that iconic movie the inexperienced youth was *Luke Skywalker*, the sidekick was *Han Solo*, the wise elder was *Obi Wan Kenobi* and so on. Another famous movie that has a very clear plot structure is *Jurassic Park*, which I've briefly deconstructed here for you;

• *Hook*: a park worker is killed by some kind of mysterious, powerful creature.
• *Inciting Event*: Doctors' Grant, who doesn't like children, and Sadler are invited to billionaire John Hammond's new theme park as professional advisors. Dinosaurs are revealed at the park.
• *Turning Point 1*: the storm arrives, and Nedry shuts down the security fences.
• *Point of No Return*: the Tyrannosaur strikes, and Dr Grant is on foot with the kids.
• *Turning Point 2*: Nedry is killed, and Dr Sadler leads the power restoration attempt as she is re–joined by Dr Grant and the kids.
• *Calamity*: the doctors and kids are cornered by the Velociraptors inside the complex. The raptors prepare to attack and rush toward the heroes…
• *Climax*: …just as the Tyrannosaur appears and attacks the Velociraptors, allowing Dr Grant to lead his friends to safety and escape the island by helicopter.
• *Denouement*: Doctor Grant is now willing to accept children in his life. John Hammond no longer wishes to genetically reproduce dinosaurs.

See how simply the structure of a two–hour movie can be broken down into these key events? This process is much easier to do backwards on a story that's already been written of course, but it's a key ability for you to develop and there's a really easy and fun way to do it.

EXERCISE 2

Watch any episode of the current crop of excellent US TV dramas currently running. Examples at the time of writing might be *The Blacklist, Game of Thrones* or *Elementary*, or from past series like *24, Castle* or *NCIS*. Have your trusty notepad handy, and as you watch the episode write down the various key points of the episode: The Hook, The Inciting Event (both of which may be the same thing!), The Point of No Return etc. Ask yourself how easy or hard it is to pick them out in each episode. Get a feel for how this reliable convention of story–telling works, so that you can confidently apply it to your own big idea.

By this point you (hopefully) have your high–concept idea ready to implement as the story anchor, you've created the main characters with whom the reader will share the journey, and you have identified or created the goal that will lead your story from its beginning to its end. This is where the fun really begins as you start to develop that singular idea into a competent and cohesive plot.

Your story idea or theme should have some element of interest attached to it, by its very nature. So, your first exercise is to think about that idea and how many other great ideas you can attach to it, each of which might represent a particular scene. These big ideas within your story are known as set pieces, and will form an extra backbone to your story.

Here's a great way of creating set pieces;

EXERCISE 3

Grab yourself a handful of coloured cards or post–it notes. Coloured cards work best because you can use red ones for villainous scenes, green or blue ones for hero's scenes and so on, making it quick and easy to spot who's doing what and where.

On each of these cards write a brief description of scenes that you think would be really exciting and relevant to your book and its central idea. For instance, when I was writing *The Identity Mine* I knew that I had an idea that involved people being able to see other people's thoughts on screens. From this starting–point I had a good think, and after a lot of pacing and mumbling to myself came up with a handful of fresh ideas and set–piece scenes around those ideas, based on this remarkable technology;

• A secret government facility where scientists and agents watched criminals in action through their own eyes and thoughts in real–time, using the evidence gathered to pre–empt major crimes. One screen is black but with little sparks of light fluttering about and strange, surreal images – the person being watched is *asleep* and we're actually witnessing their dreams.

• A good guy who murders his nearest and dearest, but is clearly devoted to them and also evidently not in control of his own actions (this became the story's hook, its first chapter).

• A scene where the intricacies of the technology mean that signals must be sent, as though the controlled person is being remotely operated – thus, those signals could potentially be intercepted or blocked, saving the day at the last moment.

• A second, disastrous scene where a hacked pilot crashes his aircraft into a ship, but awakens from his daze at the last moment – just too late!

• A scene where a scientist reveals the real–life existence of this technology, and demonstrates remote–control bees and insects being deployed (yes, it really has happened in real life!)

• A villain (terrorist) who is using all of this technology to kill, yet secretly intends to murder his final victim with his own hands – the whole build–up of murders is a ploy to draw the heroes away from his final and most important victim. The reader doesn't know about this final twist either until the last possible moment.

These are all set–piece scenes and dreaming them up helps enormously in the early stages of plotting because they represent the beginning of structure in your work. I call them story "pegs". Rather like clothes hanging on a washing line, these pegs represent key areas of your story that you can arrange in accordance with the three–act structure to get a general idea of the strongest possible layout to your novel.

Once you've generated maybe a dozen or so ideas and scenes, each one on a separate card, pick them all up and toss them onto the table in front of you, completely at random. Arrange them in a line and then just sit back and look at them.

There's a reasonable chance that within a short time you'll start to notice that the order of events could be improved by having some of the cards exchange places. Move them around a bit, experiment, see what comes up from the random placements and whether any new ideas spring from their current arrangement.

While you're doing this, it sometimes helps to have an image of the three–act structure alongside the cards, so that you can get a feel for where the scenes should come in relation to the classic methods of story–telling. There are many on the Internet that can be downloaded and printed out for you to refer to as you plot your story. The idea behind all of this is that you can, in a relatively simple series of steps, produce the first bones of structure to your story even before you've created your first character.

The Three Act Structure

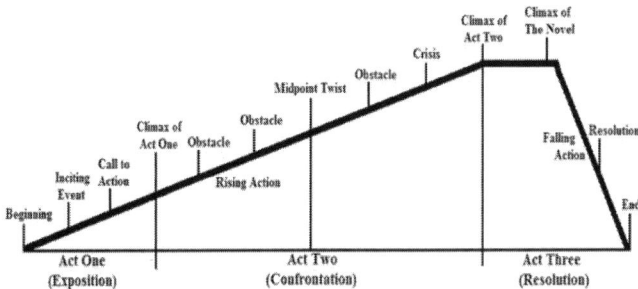

Almost every novel hangs on those main events in the three act structure: a hook, an inciting event, the first turning point when your hero truly embarks on their quest, a series of challenges before the centre of the story is reached, the Point of No Return or Midpoint Twist in the image above. Then, the story pace soars toward the second Turning Point at the climax of Act Two and the sudden failure or loss to the hero, the point where they feel as though they simply cannot carry on. Then comes the revelation, the sudden rush toward the climatic confrontation between protagonist and antagonist and then the battle is won (or perhaps lost) and the denouement takes us to the end.

One you've begun to develop these main areas of your novel, and perhaps have a few scenes in place, so the rest of the novel's scenes should start to appear naturally in your mind as you find new ways of bridging the gaps between your existing, set–piece scenes. There will be a clear need for a scene between the Inciting Event and the end of Act One, the Turning Point. You may immediately have a sense of what might be needed in that scene to continue to drive the story forward, and perhaps even who needs to appear in that scene and how many chapters it might require to cover all that's needed. This all requires some thought and time of course, but the process becomes more natural the more that you do it, and before too long it starts to become second nature.

For those of you who are devoted, life–long *pansters*, I hope that this process is relatively simple and at least allows the author an overview of the story, a God's eye perspective that allows even the most *seat–of–the–pants*author to get going without staring at that blank screen for countless hours before writing the first line.

Research

I know that it can be tempting to overdo research, because I'm as guilty of it as any author. I often get really wrapped up in intriguing theories and fascinating technologies and want to relay to the reader what I've learned.

That's all fine, but it's important to remember that you're writing a work of fiction and not a school textbook. In some cases, such as "hard" science fiction and technothrillers of the Tom Clancy variety, readers love to become embroiled in a deep description of the intricacies of an exploding nuclear bomb. In other genres, your reader will get bored and move on to another title, something that is remarkably easier to do these days on an e–reader than it was in the past when maybe they didn't have another book to read and so were forced to carry on with yours.

Things like Google Street View / Earth and other wonders of the Internet mean that there's almost nowhere than you cannot locate and describe with stunning accuracy. I know of authors who still like to jet off to other countries in order to get a sense of the place before including in in their novels – nice work if you can get it and afford it. For most of us this isn't a possibility and nor should it be a necessity. A good author's writing will give the reader the impression they've lived in the city of Delhi all their lives, even if in fact the author has never set foot in India.

Likewise, with hefty chunks of information it can be tempting to unload it all onto the reader in one go, creating an information dump (more on those later) which again will just look out of place in the scene. You may be proud of what you've learned and the effort that went into it, but ninety per cent of what you've researched shouldn't be in your novel. Most of it should be research that allows you to thoroughly *understand* what you're writing about, with the rest being the bits of highest interest that will pique the reader's curiosity and keep them turning those pages.

In short, don't let narrative details get in the way of that all–important plot.

So, after some work you will have your characters, a plot, your set–pieces and hopefully (but not necessarily) a satisfying conclusion in place. If you look at your Chapter Map, your characters and the plot and feel that something's missing, then take some more time to think about what else could happen in the story. Take long walks, think about the characters, about the plot points – figure out whether there's something missing or that the plot doesn't make sense. Remember, at the end of the story everything must have been explained and everything must make sense to the reader. Leave any stone unturned and trust me, they'll notice.

However, if you feel with some confidence that you could write your novel from what you have developed so far then it's time to switch on that computer and start typing…

If I was to focus one tenet I would suggest that authors should stick with subjects they know. Other than perhaps Tom Clancy, few have researched unfamiliar genres and developed sufficient credibility to avoid challenge. Research can never replace firsthand knowledge. Reviews in the modern world of instant feedback can be harsh and permanent so accuracy is the watch word. The former lawyer is best placed to take the reader into the courtroom and the aviator best placed to take the reader into the cockpit. An action taken in the cockpit must be accurate and credible and it is for the plot to elicit the reactions. Real life should shine through at the expense of sensationalism. At the end of a novel there can be a myriad of reactions and emotions. What I would want is for the reader to say I was there with him and to pose the question: did that really happen?

David Gledhill RAF (Ret'd) fast–jet aircrew and military thriller author.

April 2010

After eighteen months of what had seemed like endless work I had just completed my latest novel, entitled "Genesis". It was my fifth written novel and I was sure that it was my best work yet, and I hoped fervently that this treasured tome might be the one that would change my fortunes. I carefully prepared ten submission packages to the ten literary agents in London I felt best fit my genre and style, crafting my approach letter over several days, before finally posting them off and crossing my fingers that something would come of it.

A long six weeks passed by, during which three rejections slips appeared in the post. One of them had a scribble of encouragement upon it, which was more than I'd seen in terms of interaction from a literary agent for some time, but other than that there was nothing.

Then, in May, I received my latest rejection slip. I opened the letter and was about to toss it onto the living room table when I realised that it contained more than just a couple of disappointing lines. Remarkably, it was from the top literary agent in London, Luigi Bonomi, who had just been voted UK literary agent of the year. The letter was one of rejection of the novel, but not of the overall idea, and Luigi listed a series of criticisms and asked me whether I would agree to a re–write of the story based on some recommendations from him?

I nearly passed out. I must have re–read that letter a hundred times. The next day, I e–mailed Luigi and outlined what I thought I could do with the work in order to make it a better fit with what he felt publishers were looking for. Within an hour, Luigi replied by e–mail and told me that he was encouraged by my professionalism and asked if I would like to visit the offices of LBA in London for a chat?

I nearly passed out again…

VI: The terror of the blank page…

It's not unknown for some authors to sit catatonic for hours in front of a blank page, unable to start writing even if they do have a decent grasp of their plot and storyline. I have lost count of the number of times that an author has complained that they *just don't know where to start*.

The truth is that, as the author, you can start pretty much anywhere you damned well like. It's your story after all, and there are no hard and fast rules about what order you should write your chapters in. However, in twenty years of writing I have found that writing from the beginning through to the end is *generally* the best way to go about it. It should never be a chore to have to wait to get to what you perceive to be the "good bits" of your story – if it feels that there are "bad bits" to get through, then you're not ready to get started yet.

Writing fiction is easy. You just have to write a damned good first page, and then repeat that process about three hundred times.

Once you're well on your way, it's perfectly okay to skip ahead to one of your major set pieces if the intervening chapters are a bit tough to write. Sometimes, it's just something that authors need to do in order to take a break from the scene they're currently on. It's all work after all and no time spent writing is ever really wasted even if you don't like the result. It can later be edited, improved, enhanced and perfected. Furthermore, the newly created set–pieces now form a natural bridge to the prior scenes you were struggling with and ideas formed while writing the set–pieces often provide the necessary links to fill in the remaining chapters and smooth out the story.

A perfect tip for getting started on a story is not to stare at a blank screen. Did you ever find watching paint dry a stimulating process? No. Likewise, staring into space won't get you very far in a creative sense either. *Get up*, and start doing something that I've been doing ever since I started writing.

EXERCISE 4

Have a notepad alongside you and before you start writing that first chapter, *think* about it. You'll need the following details;
- The start, middle and end events of the chapter in question.
- The first line, which should be a strong hook if it's Chapter One you're writing.

• Who's in the scene, what they're doing and what their motives are.
• The *purpose* of the chapter. If it doesn't have one, you've no business writing it.

That's it, nothing more needed. If you think that the four points I've applied to a chapter's requirements are the same points I've applied to an entire novel's structure, you'd be entirely correct. Each and every chapter should read exactly like an entire novel, with a clear and distinct beginning, middle and end. Don't get caught up in the needless process of describing every little detail of your hero's surroundings unless there's a damned good reason; *i.e, they're creeping up on a serial killer or perhaps a potential victim and you want to draw out the tension as much as possible.*

So, just like your complete novel you need a hook. This is especially important in the first chapter of your book. How many people have you seen in a bookshop who pick up a novel, read the blurb on the back jacket and then open it to chapter one and read the first page? They're testing that book out, seeing if they're going to like it. If you don't grab them on that first page, you've lost them.

I like to use simple lines of dialogue as my "hook" in the first chapter of my novels. Here's a few examples of the first thing my readers see when they open my books;

"How many bodies are there?" (Apocalypse)
"She's out here somewhere." (Covenant)
'We've got him now, brother." (The Chimera Secret)
"The cold awoke her." (Survivor)
"Your time has come, Chaska." (The Nemesis Origin)

Notice what every one of those lines does? Once again it puts a *mystery* in the reader's mind: *What bodies? Who's somewhere out there, and where? Who have they got, and why? Who is Chaska and why has her time come?* Instantly the reader's natural curiosity is piqued and you've got them where you want them. Keep that sense of tension alive, that need to know, and you'll keep them turning those pages. And as the saying goes, do that for a few hundred pages more and you'll have a very satisfied reader on your hands. It sounds easy, if you say it quickly enough…

Once on your way with the first chapter, if you're lucky and like me have a very visual imagination you'll find that words will come into your mind quicker than you can type them and scenes will unfold before your eyes. But even if you don't, having a simple plan for your chapter and a beginning, middle and end firmly cemented into your mind will work wonders in drawing the story forward as you begin your journey into the book.

That's a lot of typing.

A lot of people don't give much thought to how much typing it requires to write a novel. My shortest work is probably 85,000 words long. My longest, to date, is 112, 576 words – pretty much twice the minimum generally accepted length for a book to be called a novel. An average thriller would probably come in at somewhere around the 80,000 word mark, as a rough estimate. The chances are that you're not a highly trained touch–typist – if you are, then you're well on your way. I started typing with my forefingers like a clumsy ape in 1995, and have progressed to being something of a touch–typist now although not in the classically trained sense. If I'm on a real roll I can produce over 2,000 words per hour with a small number of typos and a seriously stiff back. Such are the consequences of being a full–time author. Because I make my living from writing books, it is *essential* to put in the hours. Typically I write about 20,000 words per week during a first draft, after a week of plotting and planning. Four weeks into a project and the first draft is complete. There follows a month or so of editing, proof–reading, cover design and final polishing before the book goes out to beta–readers, street teams and such like (more on those later). As a result, I publish a new novel on average every ten to twelve weeks. That's a seriously fearsome workload for many authors, among whom even the full–timers are often quite stunned by the output.

You can't write a novel that quickly! It must be rubbish!

If I had a dollar for every time I've heard that, I'd be a very wealthy man.

The simple fact is that fast–typing alone can contribute to an author creating a novel in just a few weeks. When I was writing in my spare time as a novice, it would take two months to plot a novel, at least six months to write it (if not more) and then another six months of editing to get the damned thing into some kind of order. The long gaps between writing sessions broke up my creative flow, lines of thought were interrupted, plot lines forgotten and my typing speed was hardly stellar. A thousand words in a single day was a major achievement. The list of obstacles in part–time authorship mean that, by default, writing a competent 80,000 word novel takes a very long time.

Contrast this with my forty–hour plus week, writing full time and with decades of typing practice behind me. Even writing only 1,000 words per hour, I can realistically produce 4,000 words per day, or my normal target of 20,000 words per week. I've twenty years of novel planning, plotting, writing and editing experience behind me. I know my strengths as an author and my weaknesses and I can type pretty damned fast. Can I write a competent novel in ten to twelve weeks?

The simple answer is yes, and compared to some I'm a slow coach. Dame Barbara Cartland, probably the most prolific author of all time, wrote no less than 723 novels in her career and holds the *Guinness World Record* for the most novels published in a single year in 1983: twenty–three novels! That's almost two per month. And they were good enough to sell too – it's estimated she sold around one *billion* copies in her lifetime.

So if somebody tells you it's essential to take enormous amounts of time to write a novel, you can correct them by saying it takes enormous amounts of time to *learn to write* a novel, and that's where this book is hopefully saving you that time.

If you're a slow typist, keep practicing. You will see on your keyboard that there is a small lump on the "F" and "J" keys. They are there for touch–typing, the index finger remaining on them as the other fingers fly around the keyboard. Although a little tricky to begin with, learning to touch type now will save you countless hours in the future as you watch your novel come to life before you on the screen as your fingers move of their own accord.

But what if I'm really pressed for time?

There are options, and as ever a common–sense approach to writing can often yield spectacular results. Firstly, let's look at this issue from the perspective of an author already working full–time in their day job, or perhaps a full–time parent with little spare time (and these two criteria very likely apply to most people reading this book).

If the average novel is some 80,000 words, then one could perhaps break down the process to writing a thousand words per day. This is not quite as hard as it first might appear to an untrained typist. This book was written in Word with a layout comprising an average of two hundred and fifty words per page, the same template that I use to write my novels. Thus, a thousand words would be some four pages. However, dialogue and other formatting often reduce this per–page word count. My point is, four pages or a thousand words isn't that much to get down. If you can manage it, you'll complete a full length first–draft in about eighty days – less than three months. If five hundred words is a more manageable limit for you then you'll do it in six months, and so on. And of course the more you type the faster you'll get – once you've done the plotting and planning there really is no art to writing a novel other than sitting on your backside while getting those words down onto the page.

Dictation.

I have on my computer a program called *Dragon Naturally Speaking*. Via a microphone and some nifty software, this program allows me to simply "speak" my novels and watch the words miraculously appear on the screen before me. Needless to say, productivity leaps using this technology with 8,000 words per day a real possibility. A couple of hundred bucks buys you the *BlueTooth* version, although many authors prefer to dictate into voice recorders while walking the dog, doing the dishes, driving to work and back and so on. They then play back the recordings that evening direct to their computer's microphone.

I wrote an entire novel using *Dragon* once and although productivity was huge, so was the editing required afterward. In addition, you need a reasonably powerful computer to run the software. But for the time–limited author *Dragon* is a powerful tool that should not be overlooked, and just like typing the more you use it the better it gets.

No matter what method you use to write that first draft, the simple fact is that writing a novel will require you to spend a lot of time typing at a computer because you'll still have to edit it. If you're serious about your writing but don't think that you could get along with dictation software (I don't use mine much) then it's well worth considering a beginner's typing course. Although this represents another obstacle to overcome before sitting down and writing your first epic tome, it will pay handsome dividends in the long run: a trained touch–typist can consistently hit well over 2,000 words per hour, which means that as much of your time as possible is spent writing and not squinting at the keyboard searching for the keys.

Whatever speed you can manage I suspect it will not deter you from the craving to get started. At this time, your enthusiasm for your project will probably be overwhelming and you'll be raring to start on that first chapter. This is where a writer's discipline comes in.

Writing Discipline.

When I first started out back in 1995 I didn't have a home PC, the Internet or a cell phone. Writing was somewhat harder back then, and if I wanted to print something out I had to do it on a cranky, clattering Word Processor or take it on a 3.5" floppy disc to a print shop. Now we all have access to wonderfully fast PCs with modern word processing programs and plenty of easily affordable laptop computers with all the necessary software to write. If you're ever in need of freeware alternatives, public domain software like *Abiword* is just as capable as the more famous Microsoft Word.

For the fifteen years it took me to write a novel good enough to obtain me a publishing contract and go full–time, I had to write whenever I had the chance. For me, that meant most evenings during the week and most Sundays were my devoted writing time. While my friends were enjoying their weekends relaxing, I was slaving over a hot keyboard or making notes or taking long walks to consider storylines and characters and whatever else I might be struggling with at the time. I can recall clearly sitting in a rented room in 1996, the sun beating down outside on a glorious summer day, and telling myself the following line:

You'll enjoy other summer days much more when you're writing for a living, so keep going.

If I'm totally honest this kind of determination, while commendable, was probably too much. I should have switched off the computer and gone out and enjoyed myself for a few hours in the sunshine. While it's said that people driven

47

by high levels of discipline and motivation tend to be those who succeed, I have come to believe that it's possible to be determined and driven without denying one's self a day out in the sunshine or a night out with friends here and there. Ultimately the goal you're heading towards, that of a published author with a career ahead of them, is tough enough to attain without living like a hermit crouched over a hot laptop.

Today, I recommend a simple program based on your own life. For instance, a busy working or family life often makes it difficult to get words down on the page because it's not just about writing but being in the *mood* to write. Problems in daily life can affect creativity and make it tough to feel enthusiastic about writing, about doing another job when you've already been working all day. This is where your efforts at plotting and planning come in, giving you that storyline direction that at the very least allows you to sit down and pick up the threads with greater ease than if you were simply staring at a white screen wondering what the hell to write about. It's also where you need to get your mindset programmed correctly to view your writing not as a chore but as a joy.

EXERCISE 5

If you have enough room in your home, devote a small area of it to writing and writing *alone*. Maybe it's a spare room, a desk or just one of the seats on the couch. Maybe it's at lunchtime, or early in the morning, or at night when the kids have gone to bed. Maybe it's a half hour, or one hour or two. It doesn't matter. Set in your mind one spot that you will forever more conduct your writing until you can afford to spend more time doing it.

With your location chosen, make it as comfortable as you can. Long periods of writing can cause stress on wrists and backs, so try to ensure that you're as comfortable as you can be and take regular breaks for a walk or to do other chores. This may sound obvious but if you're successful in building a true writing career, you need to look after those wrists and back for the future.

Now, finally, buy yourself a calendar. Hang it on the wall near your writing spot, and after you've written your first days' target of X number of words or Y pages, put a tick in the date on the calendar. *Why?* Because it's a surprisingly simple and yet effective motivator. Once you've got three or four ticks up on that calendar, the desire not to fail and see an empty date is remarkably powerful.

Now, I don't someday want to hear about authors avoiding major life–saving surgery to complete the next thousand words of their novel after reading this book. Suitably essential tasks and family matters of course come first, because they're *justified* breaks in your schedule. For all other days if you've set a goal and you achieve it, keep ticking those boxes and you'll be surprised how quickly you fall into your new routine and how quickly your novel starts to grow.

May 2010

I was nervous, and I'm not normally the nervous type.

It's extremely rare for unpublished authors to find themselves in the office of a well–established agent, and there was little on the Internet describing such meetings before I had my own. Now, standing in a busy London street outside the offices of LBA Books on a hot spring morning, I was about to cross that invisible line.

Upon meeting Luigi in an office that was filled to bursting with books, he was interested initially on how long I had been writing, what about and what my day job was (I'd also been asked to send a brief C.V. in advance of the meeting). The reasoning behind this was to give Luigi a feel for where I was in my life at the time, and also to see if there was anything about me that might help to sell my novels to potential publishers and the public. Many authors write about subjects similar to their occupations, and such expert knowledge helps to encourage readers that they are going to learn something from an authority figure as well as be entertained. I was not in that position, but it obviously doesn't hinder an author if they've done what an agent considers to be a good job of their novel.

Then we got down to business. Considering the sheer volume of material Luigi handles, he recalled a great deal of detail about 'Genesis' and was able to sketch out where he felt things were letting the story down. Chief among these was pace, along with his feeling that, having started with what he called "a terrific premise", I had failed to capitalise upon it during the rest of the novel.

What followed was an hour talking over how to re–write about half of the novel in order to take full advantage of my premise, whilst trimming the novel down from its existing 150,000 words to around 110 – 120,000 words (not a small task in itself). This was to promote swifter pace within the story and also no doubt to keep potential publisher's costs down, making the title a more appealing acquisition.

Luigi made a point of remarking that one of his reasons for being willing to work with me was my own willingness to make changes based on his experience and inside knowledge of the publishing industry. We had exchanged e–mails before the meeting where he had highlighted the novel's strengths and weaknesses, and my positive responses were what prompted his invite to the LBA offices in London. He then went on to detail how he felt that male thriller–fiction was beginning to move into new directions and that I should consider following, something that I would definitely be bearing in mind as I got down to re–writing my novel to make it as commercial as possible. At no time did Luigi dictate what he felt I should do with the novel or make absolute demands – he made suggestions and then we talked them over, bouncing ideas off of each other until we found a compromise that really fitted the work. It was the first time that I'd been able to do that alongside a publishing professional and it left me bursting with new ideas.

After a hugely productive hour, Luigi told me that he would send me a standard agency agreement by e–mail that day. I was overjoyed. He then cautioned me that getting publishers to buy novels, especially in these economic hard–times was immensely difficult even for established agents and that nothing might come of this. I accepted that, but agents like Luigi don't sign an author unless he has high hopes for them, and he also said that if Genesis didn't work we'd have to find something else that did, suggesting to me that I'd entered into a business partnership that he hoped would last.

I walked out of the London office with a bounce in my step and a huge grin on my face.

After fifteen years I had prevailed and begun the next stage of my writing journey.

VII: Words, words, words...

I am only going to spend one chapter, albeit a good sized one, on the craft of writing words. This might seem a bit remiss of me considering that this is a book about writing. However, there are *entire* books dedicated to the craft of getting words down onto the page and of shaping those words the way you want them to be. What this chapter will be is a simple, easy to reference series of checks and balances that will ensure that you have something to help you both as you write and later edit your work. It's worth remembering that although there are certain well–known and reliable rules of writing that you should adhere to wherever possible in your work, ultimately your writing style will in time become your own and you should be willing to break rules if a scene *absolutely* demands it. For the most part, however, the following advice will serve any author well throughout their career.

"Show don't tell" and "avoiding adverbs"

Probably the best–known rule of creative writing is *"show don't tell"*. Don't waffle endlessly about what somebody is doing; lead the reader into their shoes as if it were *they* who is creeping about in a haunted house:

Andrea walked into the house. She opened the door and stepped into the darkness. She was utterly terrified. She managed a few more paces into the house as she heard the door close behind her. A figure appeared before her in the night, tall and ominous. Andrea knew there was nowhere left to hide.

If you found that passage a bit boring and staid, good for you – it is. Now read the next version.

Andrea crept into the house and the darkness swallowed her whole, sweat building beneath her collar and her legs unsteady. She eased forward another pace and heard the door creak shut behind her. She looked over her shoulder but could see nothing, and as she turned back a huge figure loomed from the blackness as though from hell itself. Andrea recoiled and realised that there was nowhere left to hide.

Very little has changed yet the whole paragraph reads differently. There is no reason or need to *tell* the reader that Andrea is terrified – her creeping motion, the sweat beneath her collar and unsteady legs all convey her terror without ever mentioning the word. Your reader *becomes* the character, *sees* the scene unfold as though they were themselves creeping into that house and feeling what Andrea is feeling. *Tension* is introduced into the appearance of the looming figure as it surprises Andrea, instead of just appearing without any sense of danger. There is no need to use the words *tall* or *ominous* as it becomes obvious in the prose that this is an imposing figure. Show, don't tell.

An economy of writing, the mantra of *less is more*, is perhaps the most important lesson an author can learn. It doesn't mean that once you've learned it every passage pours from your fingertips onto the page with absolute precision and perfection first time out. It simply means that when you come to edit your work you'll be a lot closer to the perfect prose you're seeking, first time around. And, as mentioned before, if your first draft is reasonably clean there becomes room for expansion and enhancement of the existing text.

As for adverbs, avoid them as much as you can.

Aaron glared at the two brothers malevolently.
Aaron glared at the two brothers and clenched his fists.

Which lines best conveys the coming confrontation?

The use of "malevolently" in the first passage is somewhat redundant as Mitchell's glare already suggests he's malevolent. Replacing it with Mitchell clenching his fists suggests impending violence and is much more effective for the reader in *showing* how Mitchell is a violent individual and that the two brothers may be in deep trouble. Although more words are used, it still remains the more effective of the two lines in terms of how the reader feels upon reading the scene.

You always know what to say: similes.

Some people have a true way with words, but it is only imagination that separates good prose from great prose.

Barny rubbed his jaw, which was thick with his beard.
Barny rubbed his heavily forested jaw.

There's not a lot between the two descriptions and yet they're miles apart in how easily the reader sees in their mind how Barny appears.

Bright thunder clouds soared above the horizon, glowing in the sunlight.
Bright thunderheads soared across the horizon like giant golden angel's wings.
Bright thunderheads soared across the distant horizon like the wings of giant golden angels.

Which one do you prefer? For me it's between lines two and three. In this case I'd go for line three: although it's a slightly longer sentence it flows more smoothly and seems more natural. Like all good writing tips, it pays to ensure that the flow of the words keeps the reader engaged in the story and not stopping in confusion as they go back and re–read a sentence.

Brian's eyes pierced her deeply.
Brian's eyes turned cold as ice.
Brian's glare chilled her to the bone.

Again, think about which one works the best. For me, eyes cannot *pierce* somebody so line one is out of the running because it makes no literal sense. Line two is better but seems a little staid. Line three is the best but it's still somewhat over–familiar, a cliché that's been used too many times: "chilled to the bone".

Brian glared at her and her blood ran like ice through her veins.

Better again. This consideration of narrative and prose is something that you'll find yourself doing throughout the process of writing a novel. It's incredibly easy to find yourself writing adverbs like *happily* or *deeply* or *hopefully*or whatever throughout the book, and the words *was* and *were* will also repeatedly rear their ugly and unnecessary heads. Don't fight them during a first draft as it's only natural and you'll slow down too much if you start editing as you go along. But when it comes to editing your first draft upon completion, learn to remove or replace those words and sentences with something a little better, a little cleaner and a little more elegant. Before long you'll realise that this process is far from laborious, and with every alteration and improvement your work will get better and better until it flows just as it should – seamlessly into the minds of your readers.

Say what now? Dialogue.

If you listen to people talking in real life they sound radically different to the way people speak on television or in novels. You might go up to somebody in the street and ask for directions, and they might not even reply for a moment as their brain races to think about where it is you're trying to get to, even if they live close by themselves.
'*Ah*, okay, right. I know, you go down there, turn right – no, *left* at the end, keeping going and *ahhh*, yeah, then you turn right and it's a half mile down on the, *errr*, on the right, by the pet shop.'
There are a lot of hesitations and thoughtful pauses in real conversations that don't need to be in the lines of dialogue within your novel. Put simply, thoughts can be directed at the reader through narrative between lines of dialogue, and the

dialogue itself should be somewhat simplified. There's a tendency for new authors to overcomplicate dialogue as per the following:

> *'Please get back down!' Sally snapped.*
> *'I don't want to!' Jenny shouted.*
> *'But it's dangerous!' Sally insisted.*
> *'I don't care, you're not my mother!' Jenny screeched vehemently.*

There are a lot of words in there designed to convey the intensity of the situation, but none of them are actually needed.

> *'Please get back down,' Sally said.*
> *'I don't want to!'*
> *'It's dangerous.'*
> *'I don't care, you're not my mother!' Jenny screeched.*

Note that in the first example the overuse of exclamation marks means that the two individuals don't sound different – their lines could be interchanged and it wouldn't change the scene. By removing them from Sally's lines in the second example, she sounds just as concerned but it's Jenny who sounds like the child and Sally the more mature friend or an adult. In addition, it's often better not to have the tag lines after the lines of dialogue *if* they can be avoided. The flow of the conversation and the way in which the characters speak should make it easy for the reader to know who is speaking at any one time without having to constantly add their names to the relevant lines. Likewise, *snapped*, *shouted* and *insisted* can all be removed without compromising the scene's intensity or the clarity of the characters' differing personalities.

Although my example is a very simple one, such smart editing and cleaning up of dialogue can be applied to even the most complex of scenes. *Less is more*. But what about actions? Can they be used to convey a character's emotions without them having to speak a single word? Of course they can.

Look at the example below.

> *Jason stood in the darkness of the parking lot, a knife grasped tightly in his hand. Four men were arrayed before him, steel blades flickering in the night and a figure kneeling between them with a hood pulled over their head.*
> *'Release her,' Jason said.*
> *'Do you have the money?' one of the four men said.*
> *'It's here,' Jason replied. 'It's yours as soon as she's free.'*
> *'Show us or I'll cut her throat right here and now.'*
> *Jason's grip on his knife tightened and he swallowed.*
> *'He's scared,' one of the men sneered.*
> *'Or he doesn't have the cash,' said another, dark eyes glaring at Jason.*
> *Jason's took an involuntary step back as his blood ran cold through his veins.*

Note that Jason hasn't revealed a thing to the reader about the money he may or may not have, but his actions have clearly conveyed that he's probably bluffing and that he's afraid that the kidnappers have seen through him. Did the line *"a knife grasped tightly in his hand"* convey to you that he might be scared already?

Small things can make big differences in narrative and dialogue. One very good way to check that you're getting somebody's voice and character right is to swap lines with another character in your book. Read a page or so of the altered lines and see if the characters still sound the same. If you cannot tell between them, then you need to define your characters more clearly to ensure that the reader can tell them apart without constant references to their name or what they're doing.

He did what?!

Many authors seem to struggle with characterization and dialogue for understandable reasons: it's in our nature to write characters who think and act as *we* would do, and those personal instincts often make it onto the page so that the author's characters all seem to be the same. A handy tip for dialogue is to think about your friends, and people you've known over the years, and think about how they sounded to you. Do you think that you could swap their dialogue and still have it sound natural? Could you take the words, mannerisms, swagger and anger of the loudest and most aggressive person you've ever known and transplant them into the meekest, most nervous person you've ever known and have it sound natural? Of course you couldn't.

EXERCISE 6

I want you to write a short scene. Before you do so, I want you to think about something that you really *hate*. Perhaps you're a vegetarian who hates processed meat. Maybe you're a cyclist who hates cars, or a Democrat who cannot understand the viewpoint of a Republican.

Now, I want you to write a scene about an argument or debate between two characters; one whose points of view you agree with, and one who opposes everything that you stand for. I want you to write this scene so that your enemy *convincingly wins* the debate, without cruelty or cheating or becoming the villain of the piece in any way. You must conceive of a way that they could beat you while sounding completely different to you and standing for the opposite of what you believe.

Being able to write characters who don't sound like you, the author, is one of the greatest steps to producing solid, believable characters who will be memorable to your readers long after they finish the final page.

So, each character in your book must sound and act differently to a sufficient extent that you could not transplant their dialogue on the page and have it sound right. Here's a simple example:

"Good morning, you're looking well. Would you like a coffee?'
"What's good about it? Where's my itinerary? Two sugars and make it fast!'

It shouldn't be too hard to figure out the nature, or mood, of the two characters in the above lines. Notice that at no point have I revealed either of the characters' sex, age, height, build or anything else. Neither have I used the words happily, angrily or any other words that end in *"ly"*. It's a reasonable bet though that when you read it you saw in your mind an office, a secretary, an angry boss and a really bad start to everybody's day.

Less is more.

These are the fundamentals of writing both dialogue and character. Novice authors have a natural tendency to want to describe every single thing in the room before they get down to the business of writing the scene, because they think that it's essential to the reader's sense of where they are and in whose company. The truth is that most readers just want to know what's going on in the clearest way possible, not what colour the flowers in the vase on the window sill are, or what somebody's wearing. This is worth repeating yet again in large capitals (I know, steady on there Dean,) because it's very important:

LESS IS MORE.

I'm not going to write a large paragraph of boring exposition in order to further justify what I mean, which is what a lot of authors of these kinds of books like to do in order to show you how clever they (think) they are. Instead, here's the scene again with a little bit more detail but still well within the boundaries of *less is more*:

Marshall saw the precinct door open and Captain Agry barrel through it, her suit in disarray and her hair a tangled mess in stark contrast to her normally pristine appearance. Peter folded his hands together before him and put on a bright smile.

"Good morning, you're looking well today. Can I get you a coffee?"

Agry rolled her bloodshot eyes at Marshall as she stormed by in a haze of alcohol fumes. She crashed through her office door to see the normally perfectly–ordered desk inside strewn with debris from last night's post–arrest party.

"What's good about it? Where's my itinerary? Two sugars and make it fast.'

Marshall stifled the grin on his face and strolled across to the coffee machine as Agry slammed her door behind her.

Just a couple of lines added and the entire scene's nature is changed from one of an aggressive confrontation to one of almost comradely banter. The instinctive choice of sex for each character has been deliberately switched with just the changing of a few words, and the addition of references to something involving alcohol happening last night further alters the nature of the confrontation. Most importantly, their dialogue hasn't changed – it's still clear who is the more naturally aggressive of the pair by the way that they've chosen to speak. If that's just because one character has a hangover and the other doesn't, so be it, but it's still clear and you couldn't switch the dialogue and make the scene work.

Another small hint: the character who is most angry has been given the surname *Agry*, just one letter short of the word "angry". This is a subliminal piece of writing psychology which I try to practice occasionally. The protagonist in my *Warner & Lopez* series, Ethan Warner, has such a surname because he works for the government and is a former Marine and investigative journalist whose skills are often used to *warn* people of dangerous events. A villainous character I had in a thriller was a cruel, greedy oil billionaire named Dwight. G. Oppenheimer. In real life, J. Robert Oppenheimer was the name of a scientist involved in America's nuclear programme. He wasn't at all a cruel man by nature, but his name became synonymous with the destructive power of the nuclear age: *"Now I am become death, the destroyer of worlds."* While I wouldn't recommend overusing this particular little naming trick, it does come in handy when you want to subliminally convey the identity of your novel's chief villain (or lure the reader into *thinking* that they're the villain when in fact they will become a hero later on – dual thinking!).

Using slang, accent and dialect.

Some authors have a canny ear for the tone of regional dialect, and others do not. Most of the time it's fine just to use the narrative and description of your character to convey to the reader how they sound.

'I don't care, I'm going into town,' Philippa droned in her nasal, monotone South African dialect.

However, it is also worth making the effort to drop in the occasional phonetic word or two to bring the character's dialogue to life when it feels right to do so.

'I don't *keer*, I'm going into town,' Philippa droned.

This helps refresh the reader's memory of a character's accent without labouring the point or filling line after line with unreadable streams of phonetics. Contrary to what you might think, people read their own language and dialect fluidly and generally prefer normal prose. If strange phonetics start appearing all over the place it really slows things down. Keep it simple and effective: less is more.

The same goes for slang: well used, this can be extremely effective in conveying somebody's background, upbringing and even their race before they've been described to the reader.

> *Michael spotted the informant, crossed the street and got in his face.*
> *'Are you Connor Jackson?' he demanded.*
> *The informant turned without concern.*
> *'Yo brudda, who's askin'?'*

Pretty good chance that in one line you've got an (admittedly stereotyped) image in your mind about the informant's race and general appearance. It's again a simplistic but effective example of how you can illuminate in the reader's mind the appearance and character of a new player in your scene without resorting to a paragraph of exposition about their clothes, looks, history and so on. Keep it simple.

Character composition.

As a final note on character, dialogue and how to present the players in your story, it's worthwhile drawing up a simple "character ladder". This can be as short as you wish and it can be useful in reminding yourself how a character looks, sounds and moves to ensure that they stand out clearly and consistently throughout your novel. I use a post–it note and stick it to my monitor when working on a character's early scenes, to check that I'm portraying them right.

Such a ladder might list height, weight, colour, financial status and a few other pertinent details that will help you each time you come to write scenes for them. I sometimes add a line of their favourite dialogue or a personal catch–phrase that brings them to life in my mind, just like they will spring to life in the reader's mind.

> 'What do we got?' – Detective Tyrell, *Covenant.*
> 'You'll have to see that to believe it.' – Doug Jarvis, *Warner & Lopez* series.

Aaron Mitchell, an assassin in my *Warner & Lopez* series, is physically imposing and speaks in a drawl that is somewhat hypnotic to characters and yet conveys danger. Some characters could have a slight defect perhaps, a limp, colour blindness, nervous ticks or other quirks that help them to stand out. Usually these sorts of things are best reserved for secondary characters, those who don't appear often in the novel and so need something to really remind the reader of who they are and what they look like. These quirks serve excellently to jog the memory of the reader through association and prevent the all–important flow of the novel from breaking up as they try to remember who the hell Quentin Hurrell's sister from Wisconsin was.

So, with your writing method considered, it's time to get typing and start thinking about how you're going to approach the major scenes step–by–step in your book.

Summer 2010

One of my first experiences of professional editing advice was the unenviable task of reducing my 150,000 word novel Genesis to around 100,000 words while also conducting a major structural edit based on my literary agent's advice. The work took me three months during the summer of 2010 and was done while sitting on our bed in my wife's one–bedroom apartment, after work, on a cheap laptop while she plied me with coffee.

This twelve–week marathon resulted in some serious back–ache, square eyes and a desire to never, ever see a single page of my novel Genesis again after the fourth read–through of the entire book. The relief when I finished in August 2010 was enormous, as though I could finally relax again and maybe take a little time off for myself even though the summer was almost over. I finished the project and with a sudden sense of anxiety that I'd forgotten to do something I spent another weekend poring over my notes, checking chapters, checking notes again, checking chapters yet again and generally reducing myself to a quivering wreck before finally sending the completed file off to Luigi one Sunday evening.

I then collapsed onto the sofa and drank beer.

It was two or three long days of wondering and worrying before Luigi wrote back to me, and when he did I was again off on the Euphoria Train as he lauded how well I'd done and what a transformation the book had undergone. After a few e–mails back and forth, during which Luigi reminded me not to get too excited and that selling books was a very tough thing to do in the current market, he said that he was sending the manuscript out to nine of the world's largest publishing houses that very afternoon.

I drank more beer.

In fact my wife and I went out for dinner to celebrate, and for the first time in fifteen years it seemed as though I was finally going to get the break that I'd worked so long and so hard for. For once it wasn't going to be the "other guy" who got the deal: this time, it was going to be me.

I went to work the next day bursting with the desire to shout out to the whole world that I was about to become a published author, but I had to hold it all inside because there was no deal yet and I couldn't afford to let my boss know about what had happened. Still, it seemed as though the world was on my side. I had beaten countless thousands of others to the finish line and was within inches of victory, my wife was three months pregnant with our daughter and everything was going fine. I had a good job and so did Debbie. The future was bright.

I got to work, parked my motorcycle, walked inside and my boss called me in and sat me down.

'I'm sorry Dean, but I'm going to have to make you redundant.'

VIII: The best and the worst of things: major plot points.

A staple of all fiction is the *moment of crisis*. In a typical novel or movie, there will be several of these and they should all include *CONFLICT, TENSION* and *EMOTION* for your characters. As per the three–act–structure, each successive moment of crisis (also sometimes called *pinch points*) must have increasingly higher stakes for your protagonist and, ideally, for all of your characters. It's worth remembering that although the motivations of your protagonist and antagonist are diametrically opposed, their mutual goals must both still point toward the inevitable confrontation at the story's climax. Therefore, their respective journeys must be inextricably linked.

Although there can be quite a few moments of crisis within your novel, there are those that are most crucial to the story and they come at easily definable points;

1. The Inciting Event
2. Turning Point One
3. The Point of No Return
4. Turning Point Two
5. Climax and Confrontation

Between these major points come smaller moments of tension, perhaps evenly spaced between the moments of crisis which often are represented by major set piece scenes. However, your story hangs by its major moments of crisis and these are worth delving into in more detail.

The Inciting Event.

Having opened your story with a memorable and intriguing hook, now comes the task of introducing your protagonist and the lead–up to the inciting event. This is where we see your hero's normal world, just prior to the major inciting event that will send them on their new journey toward the climax of your story.

There are many ways this can be done. Some stories get to the inciting event very quickly, others take longer. The beats and pace of your novel should, if you have a decent plot in place, dictate where and when the inciting event should best occur.

Examples

The inciting event from *Jurassic Park* is the moment when John Hammond arrives at the dig site of Doctor Grant and Doctor Sadler, and invites them to survey a spectacular and (at this stage in the story) mysterious wildlife park he has built off the coast of Costa Rica.

The inciting event in *Star Wars* is when Obi–Wan–Kenobi invites Luke Skywalker to accompany him to Alderaan after viewing Princess Leia's holographic plea for help.

The inciting event in *Raiders of the Lost Ark* is when Dr Marcus Brody takes Indy to meet the Army representatives, who reveal that the Nazis have found Tanis, the supposed resting place of the lost Ark of the Covenant.

Your Inciting Event should represent a clear and present danger or incentive for your protagonist to embark upon their journey, perhaps reluctantly at first but with ever increasing vigour.

Turning Point One

Your protagonist arrives at the first major *crisis point*. This is the moment when they must decide whether they will continue on with their journey. They must of course, otherwise the story would be over, but their deliberations must be convincing to the reader. The reader must *want* them to continue on, but their concerns or the obstacles to their path must be understandable and believable. Perhaps the murder of an ally provokes them to continue on, or new information that makes pursuing a killer possible when it wasn't before. Either way, your protagonist *must* decide to push on against the forces arrayed against them.

Point of No Return

The protagonist reaches the biggest crossroads of the story. This is the point where, once committed, it would be impossible to go back to how things were at the beginning of the story. The protagonist must know this and must be aware that moving forward will raise the stakes even higher, and could likely risk losing their life if they continue on. High stakes at this moment are very important – the reader must *believe* that your hero is sufficiently motivated to risk everything to achieve their goal.

The PONR can also refer to an event where the protagonist is unable to return due to forces beyond their control.

Examples

In *Jurassic Park*, the Point of No Return is the Tyrannosaur's violent and thrilling escape from its paddock after Nedry shuts down the power, an act which throws Dr Grant into the jungle with two children. Dr Grant is now forced to proceed on foot on a dinosaur infested island with two vulnerable children by his side, both of which are problems his character would much rather do without.

In *Star Wars*, the capture of Han Solo's *Millennium Falcon* by the Death Star forces Luke Skywalker into direct conflict with the Empire, and also gives him the chance to rescue the imprisoned Princess Leia.

In *Despicable Me*, the Point of No Return is when Gru is turned down by the Bank of Evil for money to build his moon–stealing rocket. The girls offer him what little they possess to help, and Gru is on his way again as the Minions likewise offer money and assemble to build the rocket with whatever they can find.

Turning Point Two

The second turning point in any novel is generally one of the highest moments of tension of any story, followed by the lowest point for the hero. This is the moment where the hero has laboured ever upward on their quest from the Point of No Return. They have fought back against their oppressor (or sought to be with their one true love, or become determined to achieve the impossible by whatever means necessary) and are almost at the point where they can achieve victory!

Thus, this is the precise moment where everything *MUST* fall apart.

One of the great staples of storytelling is the sudden twist, the unexpected calamity that unfolds at the last moment the reader expects and plunges the hero into depths of despair from which it must be quite conceivable to the reader that they will never return. This is where the importance of plotting comes in: the sudden and overwhelming defeat must be both devastating *and believable*. It is no good having your valiant, muscular hero standing tall and invincible before the army of the enemy and then succumbing to a sudden and unexpected sneezing fit that costs him the war. Unless it's a comedy. Or about cocaine. Or both.

Some writers find that they struggle with conceiving of a calamity suitable enough to warrant the scene, but I find that it's all part of the fun of constructing the story. It is quite likely that through the writing of the preceding chapters you, the author, will realise that the rug–pulling moment was there all along, that the solution will present itself as the threads of your story close in on each other in those final, racing chapters to the end. Whatever that rug–pulling moment becomes for you, it must appear to the reader that there can be no escape for your hero, that they are doomed and that nobody can rescue them.

Examples of the rug–pulling moment and the following rise to victory:

Star Wars: *Luke Skywalker is flying down the Death Star's trench, all of his wingmen are dead and Darth Vader is right behind him, flanked by two more Tie Fighters, his thumb on the trigger as he takes aim. There is nobody left to help Luke as Han Solo has abandoned him, and with all other fighters destroyed or having fled there is no way to defend himself. Darth Vader takes careful aim and squeezes the trigger…*

.. when out of the flare of a nearby sun comes the Millenium Falcon, Han Solo hooting with joy during his surprise attack as he opens fire and sends Vader and his wingmen spinning out of control into space.

Raiders of the Lost Ark: *Indy and Marion have been captured by the Nazis and are tied to a post, unable to escape as Belloq and his countless Nazi conspirators open the legendary Ark of the Covenant. From within the Ark soar demons and ghosts, and it seems as though the Nazis have conquered the fabled weapon and will go on to win the war. Indy tells Marion to close her eyes, that they shouldn't look upon the wrath of God…*

… as suddenly the Ark's ghosts turn savage and the entire area is scoured of life by flames, the wrath of God on Earth. Indy and Marion, innocent bystanders, keep their eyes shut tight and are spared the destruction, the flames freeing them from their bonds as the Ark seals itself once more.

Jurassic Park: *Doctor Grant and Sadler are trapped in the park museum with two children, cornered by a pair of vicious Velociraptors. Both exits are blocked by the predators and there is no longer any escape. Grant shields the children and Sadler uselessly with his body, frozen in place as the velociraptor before them coils its legs and leaps to strike…*

… when from the half–built rear entrance of the museum lunges the enormous Tyrannosaurus Rex, seeing only the moving velociraptors. The huge predator snatches both of the 'raptors up and kills them as Grant sneaks by with Sadler and the children to flee for freedom and safety.

It is worth reiterating the importance of the *duality* of scenes. It is all part of the *conflict* that is essential to all storytelling that you should always strive to ensure that when your hero is experiencing the *worst* of times, then the *best* of things should happen to them and vice versa. Any story that merely features one event following another without any sense of contrast or conflict is ultimately doomed to be boring and staid: it is conflict that drives a story and the emotions of the reader, which is why so many double–act stories feature characters who are on the same side but diametrically opposed in their characters and methods. *Chalk and cheese*, as they say. The contrast provides both entertainment for the reader and opportunities for conflict among those characters as they variously betray or uplift each other as the story progresses.

Remember: the greater the stakes in your hero's journey, the greater the rug–pulling moment becomes. However, the greater their fall at that moment, the harder it must be for them to pick themselves up and again strive for their ultimate goal. Tension, conflict and high stakes are the tools of your trade whether you're writing a romance, a thriller or science–fiction.

EXERCISE 7

Examine your story's plot and seek locations where, when things are going really well for your hero, you can create a scene where the worst possible thing unexpectedly happens to them. Then find a scene where everything's gone to hell for your protagonist, and seek a way for something incredibly good to unexpectedly happen to them.

These moments in your story can become hugely memorable for readers and affect them emotionally. Use them wisely and always seek opportunities for them.

September 2010

I'll never forget the two weeks after September 9th, 2010. Having been made redundant on the same day my manuscript went out to publishers for auction, I spent a couple of days hunting for jobs. I didn't tell Luigi that I'd lost my job because I didn't want to influence his decisions on what offers from publishers, if we got any, to accept. I decided to wait it out and see what happened.

I'd gone from feeling on top of the world to worrying how on earth I was going to support my pregnant wife and future daughter without a job. The country had been plunged into recession along with the rest of the western world and I didn't dare hope that any book deal I might get would save us. My wife was a scientist and had a great job but even her company was suffering the effects of the economic crash. Suddenly, our future once again looked uncertain.

I heard nothing from Luigi in a deafening silence that lasted for days. Then, finally, a text from him one evening:

"Transworld and Harper Collins turned it down."

I went to bed that night with shoulders slumped and with concerns weighing heavily on my mind. I think that I was resigned to the fact that perhaps I had been too hasty in assuming that a book deal would ever emerge from this whole charade, that Covenant was good enough at all for the big publishing houses.

The next morning I awoke to a fresh text from Luigi and reluctantly opened it.

"Pan Mac offering £150,000 for three. Waiting to hear from S&S. Turned down £100,000 from them as not enough."

My heart skipped a few beats as I stared at the phone. A hundred fifty grand?! NO WAY?!

I phoned my wife, who was at work, and told her what had happened. Debbie couldn't believe it either. From that moment on, everything was a blur that lasted several days.

Pan MacMillan had offered the £100,000 for three books, as had Simon & Schuster, and Luigi had turned them both down flat (but didn't tell me about it until afterward). He knew that they were fishing for a quick sale and he decided to wait for the other publishers to get back to him. It was a huge offer for three books from a debut author and had I been un–agented I would have been tempted by it, given my unemployment at that time. That was the advantage of having an expert literary agent on my side.

A week later and offers from Simon & Schuster, Pan Mac and others kept coming in, each publisher trying to outbid the other as Luigi skilfully played one publisher off another. Forced into a much sought–after blind auction, Simon & Schuster went to their American editors for more money, and two nail–biting weeks of waiting finally ended on a Monday morning when Luigi sent me the text that finally changed my life.

"Accepted final offer from S&S: £350,000 for worldwide rights for three. Well done!"

It doesn't happen to many authors, and it doesn't happen often for those that do find themselves on the end of a dream deal. After fifteen years of hard graft I'd finally broken through with a major international deal and I stopped looking for other jobs. I didn't need them because, unbelievably, I'd done it.

I could now call myself a professional author.

IX: Quicken the pace and cut to the chase.

Writing a novel isn't a sprint, it's a marathon. By definition of nothing more than the sheer number of words required to write a novel, it takes a while. Even working full–time and writing 4,000 words per day, it can take me a month to write a first–draft of a new novel. An author writing in their spare hours might take months or even a year to complete a first draft, and that can create issues with the novel's pace.

The generally accepted length for a fiction novel is somewhere between 75,000 and 120,000 words. Some genres such as fantasy can run much longer than that, others like Young Adult should remain at the lower end of the scale, with 50,000 words being acceptable. Science fiction also tends to be on the longer side. There is no truly hard and fast rule about length, and generally your book should already be well formed enough in your mind that you have a sense of how long it should be.

Within that overall word count will be the chapters themselves. These can have an extraordinary effect on a reader's sense of pace. For instance, I typically write chapters that are six pages in length, with a word count of about 1,500 words. The reason for this is that I write thrillers and the essence of such books is to keep the reader *turning those pages*. If the chapters are extremely long, the reader might not want to commit to another one if they're tired or perhaps have other things to do. Shorter chapters allow them to read "just one more" before turning out the light or heading off to pick the kids up from school. That factor alone can increase the sense of excitement and pace for the reader.

James Patterson is perhaps the most well–known author who uses this method, some would say to the extremes as many of his chapters are less than two pages in length! In contrast, Lee Child's chapters often seem to go on for an age, although his readers clearly don't mind. Use a mixture of common sense and the needs of the scene you're writing to judge when to bring things to a close, and if a chapter really does seem like it's going on for too long, consider splitting it into two. You might even be able to get one of those all–important mini-cliff hangers in somewhere at the end of the first chapter to keep the reader turning the pages into the second.

Pacing in scenes

Differing scenes will require differing pace in order to keep teasing at the reader's emotions and anxiety in order to make the best of each of those scenes. For instance, if your character is a cop who is about to enter an abandoned building in which something terrible has occurred, you want to drag that scene out a bit to increase the tension.

Tyrell rushed forward into the darkened maw of the house.
'Police! Stay where you are!'
Tyrell's voice was muted by the narrow hallway ahead, lost in deep shadows. He crept forward into the darkness, Lopez close behind. An intense blanket of heat cloaked the inside of the house, sweat drenching his skin and trickling beneath his shirt.
'Police! Stay still, face down on the floor!'
The silence taunted him as he caught the sickly–sweet aroma of putrefaction drifting on the air. The walls of the hall were bare but for a few tattered scraps of paper hanging entombed in gossamer webs, the carpet thin and caked in the filth of ages. Tyrell advanced toward a passage at the end of the hall that opened left and right.

Dean Crawford, *"Covenant"*

The cause of the bad odours is not yet revealed, but the focus is instead on Tyrell's surroundings and the emotions they create as he moves forward. Shown, not told, this increases the reader's excitement and tension as they await the inevitable scene that must lay somewhere in the house.

In contrast, an author should seek to accelerate the pace of the narrative as the characters enter an action scene. Here, the emphasis shifts to a rapid series of events interspersed by very brief details about their surroundings to keep the scene alive in the reader's mind.

Ethan plunged out of the cloud alongside Vladimir, who was grasping for the bundle falling beside him. He grabbed it with one hand and directed a savage grin of victory at Ethan before he pulled his chute cord again. The drogue chute billowed open above them with an audible boom as Ethan saw the Russian shoot away under the immense deceleration, but almost immediately the chute tore apart with a thunderous crack.

Vladimir screamed as he fell alongside the burial shroud and plummeted towards the rocks of the river below. Ethan rolled over and extended his arms and legs as his suit once again generated lift and he soared away. He found his gaze fixed upon the Russian as he plunged the last few hundred feet toward the floor of the gorge and then his body smashed into the rocks with an audible crunch and disintegrated upon impact in a dark flare of crimson blood.

Dean Crawford, *"The Nemesis Origin"*

One can use longer sentences in action sequences, almost making the reader breathless as they sense the quickening pace of the scene. Events are more immediate in their execution, nothing being dwelled on for too long as the action sequence unfolds before the reader.

We will deal with action sequences in more detail later, but for now we will stay with the subject of pace and focus on two of the most overlooked factors in the art of writing truly page–turning scenes.

MYSTERY AND FLOW

Look at that, it's so important I went all *capitally* again. Mystery and flow represent two of the most important factors of all fiction, so are worth dealing with separately.

Flow

The flow of a story I'm sure is something you're familiar with as a reader, although you might not be aware of it. For instance, have you ever been reading a book and suddenly from the distant universe you hear your phone ringing or somebody knocking at the door? It was as though you were *so far gone* into the world of the book you were reading that you had lost all connection with the real world.

Firstly, if that has happened to you then re–read the book in question because the author clearly had done a very good job. Secondly, the novel's flow was so perfect that you were entirely engrossed within it. Conversely, have you ever been reading a great book and then something that didn't fit jerked you out of that comfortable, mesmerising read? The flow of the story was interrupted and the trance spoiled.

A book's flow must be smooth, flawless, like a perfect river of information streamed directly into the reader's imagination so that nothing else commands their attention. Your hard work on narrative, dialogue, editing, plotting and all of the many other tasks that writing a novel involves will help smooth the story telling flow and keep the reader moving ever–forward toward the climax. Thus, no paragraph must be too long, no dialogue too stilted, no character too ill–defined.

Your mission is always, and forever will be, to create the perfectly flowing novel through attentive editing and continuous practice.

Writing Tip:

Finish your day's writing when you're half–way through a chapter.

This may seem like a bit of an odd thing to do – why finish when you're on a roll? It's a part of human instinct to finish what we started. However, if you're on a roll sometimes that's the best place to stop (provided it's roughly at the end of your working day). This is simply because the next time you sit down to write it will be much easier to pick up the threads and continue onward at the *same pace*. If you're already racing along and in the middle of a great scene, you're likely to find it much easier to recapture that feeling after a day or more away from your novel. However, if you work late to complete a chapter and the next day you're staring at a blank page again, it can hold you up as you try to think about where you're going next.

Mystery

It can become tough for an author to know how much and how soon to reveal details of their character's mission. The long duration of a first–draft can produce narrative and dialogue that goes on and on and on and on… Picking up the threads of last night's or even last week's work breaks the flow of the story in much the same way for an author as it will for a reader. This is where care over some basic planning earlier in the process does allow the author to keep an eye on the length of chapters and the overall book itself, but most important of all it teaches the author to keep thinking about the most important factors in the writing of the novel, of which mystery is one.

Keep your cards close to your chest!

Imagine if the movie *Raiders of the Lost Ark* had begun with the Nazis finding and opening the Ark. It wouldn't have been much of a movie for the next ninety minutes, would it? Whatever your story central idea is, whether it be the hunt for a serial killer, the discovery of some world–shattering icon or a quest for true love, you must *make the reader wait*. Mystery is one of the main reasons why the reader continues to turn the page, and when it comes to most books the more mysteries you can reasonably include the better.

By mysteries I don't necessarily mean *"who killed victim X?"* A mystery can be invoked with a single line. Look at the example below, intended to be the first lines of a crime novel:

Detective Byron Samson turned away from the brutal homicide, his hands
shoved into his pockets against the cold as he rubbed a golden broach grasped
inside his right hand.
*   'How long since we found the bodies?' he asked a nearby forensics officer*
working the scene.
*   A cell phone buzzed in Samson's pocket, and not for the first time that day he*
ignored it as the forensics officer replied.

What brutal homicide? What's the significance of the golden broach Detective
Samson rubs in his hand? Bodies? How many are there? Who is calling him and
why is he ignoring those calls?

Four mysteries, all at once. The reader's going to want to know about all of
them, so as the author you must tease them along. Keep secrets, horde them if you
want, but if you do then you cannot deny the reader the pay–offs as the end.

Some mysteries, such as the contents of the ancient cryptex in Dan
Brown's *The Da Vinci Code*, were kept a secret until the very end of the novel.
Likewise, Steven Spielberg and screenwriter Lawrence Kasdan wisely kept the
scene where the Ark of the Covenant is opened until the end of *Raiders of the Lost
Ark*. In contrast, the dinosaurs of *Jurassic Park* were revealed at Turning Point
One, but mysteries were kept revealing *how* the dinosaurs were created until much
later.

Where mysteries are presented and resolved depends very much on the details
of your own particular novel. What must be consistent though is the fact that
mysteries exist within the story and that they are *fully* resolved by the end of your
novel, a process known as "plants and pay–offs".

Plants and pay offs.

All works of fiction revolve their plot and sub–plot around *plants* and *pay–offs*.
These represent those subtle hints, those tangible signs of mystery such as
Detective Samson's golden broach featured above. But if you introduce such a
plant like the broach then you *must* ultimately give the reader the satisfaction of the
pay–off, revealing the significance of the broach and what it means to Detective
Samson. Failure to do this can upset readers as it then represents an unfinished
thread in the story, and stories don't like unfinished threads and plot holes. (This
can be ignored if the pay–off is something that will come in a later novel in a
series, whereby the mystery is retained somewhat to convince the reader to buy the
next book. Be careful though, that if you do this you do it *very well* and don't
disappoint the reader and lose their next purchase). The story must be complete
and self–contained, the retained mystery a new one that will be continued in book
two.

Continuity.

One of the greatest failures to accurately complete a pay–off, and thus continuity, was seen in the movie *Jurassic Park*. Having been shown the Tyrannosaur Paddock during daylight, filled with dense jungle behind massive fences and yet with no T–Rex in sight, the audience knows for sure that the apex–predator is in there somewhere. We see a goat introduced in an attempt to coax the T–Rex out but it doesn't work and the tour moves on, disappointed. The *plant* has been made…

Later in the movie, the tour vehicles break down at night outside the same paddock. The goat is gone, the T–Rex storms in and everything goes to hell. *Pay off* complete, right?

Well, yes and no. After the fences come down the T–Rex pushes one of the tour cars into its enclosure, but now instead of dense jungle there's a fifty–foot concrete cliff down which our intrepid heroes are forced to flee. This cliff has appeared at the same spot where the T–Rex appeared. Either the six–tonne dinosaur miraculously levitated over this plunging abyss or it's the mother of all continuity errors.

Continuity is important for obvious reasons, and it's where at least a *modicum* of plotting and planning before writing the first draft of a novel comes into play. Having certain crucial aspects of the story mapped out before putting finger to keyboard ensures that the majority of errors in continuity can be avoided, reducing the headache of trying to match everything up later in the story.

Many of my own novels are of the globe–trotting variety, and even with proper planning I've spent many an hour working out time zones to ensure that when it's daylight in the novel on one continent, it's night time in another. When a novel is tightly plotted or relying on a time–line to make the plot tick, getting these details right is essential because, trust me, there are millions of readers out there and if you make a mistake they'll notice. *You* would, wouldn't you?

November 2011

"Fortune and glory, kid. Fortune and glory."
Indiana Jones and the Temple of Doom

It's weird to have a dream unrealised for fifteen years and then suddenly see it all come together. After months of editing and meetings at Simon & Schuster UK in London, my cherished debut Covenant hit the bookshelves in November 2011, a full year after the contract had been signed.

"To see your name in lights" is something that people often talk about, but when it happens for real and on a truly grand scale it's something that's hard to convey. My book appeared on the CBS Action Channel as an advert "sponsoring" episodes of "24", the hit Kiefer Sutherland action drama. Train stations across cities in the UK had large displays featuring the book's cover. I got texts from friends in New York City, USA, showing my book on display on the shelves between Michael Crichton and Lee Child, and from others holidaying around the world. I did countless interviews and was invited to parties where I rubbed shoulders with everyone from Danni Minogue to the late Terry Wogan, from Paul Gascoigne to Arnold Schwarzenegger. The whole experience was something of a blur and to be honest I never quite warmed to it. Everybody was extremely welcoming and it really felt as though I'd "arrived", but I was closing in on forty years old so I suppose four decades of not being invited to celebrity parties had kind of taken the edge off it for me.

Positive reviews for the novel flooded in from publications like The Wall Street Journal, Melbourne Age, The Sun, The Guardian and others. Through 2012 two more books in the series were released, Immortal and Apocalypse, and on the strength of my books hitting The Sunday Times paperback best seller list Simon & Schuster UK bought two more books in the series. The rights for the two further titles in the UK and Commonwealth went for £100,000.

I was, to say the least, riding high on the crest of a towering wave of literary invincibility. My wife and I bought a new home and settled in, investing some of the advance money to improve the house and better our future and that of our daughter, Emma. The rest we carefully saved, ever cautious that the entertainment industry is a fickle beast and that fame can come and go as easily as the ebbing of the seasons and tides.

As it turned out, that was the best thing we could have done.

X: Action!

Boom!

So, it's time to write your first action sequence. For many authors the thrust and parry of a major chase and action sequence is where the real writing happens, when the flow of the fingers over the keys is the fastest and the most work can be done in the shortest amount of time. For me this is especially true, but it has to be said that an author must still have a plan in place: writing an endless chase sequence will just exhaust your reader, so thought must go into how you're going to play this sequence out.

An action sequence also does not have to involve vehicles, blazing guns and so on. Action simply means characters acting with *great purpose* under conditions of *great stress*. The scene in question should contain all of the tension and conflict that you've been learning about so far, distilled into a single action scene with laser–guided precision.

The tension should be built so that just as you think the hero is going to achieve their goal, something else gets in the way. This can be achieved as easily in a scene with a bomb that needs defusing as it can with two runaway vehicles hurtling down a highway exchanging gunfire. People acting with *great purpose* where the stakes are high is all that matters.

Scene length

Action scenes are high in tension and pace so they can be quite exhausting for a reader if they go on too long. As stated in a previous chapter I usually aim for chapters that are approximately 1,500 words long. This equates to about six pages in a normal Word document. There should never be a set rule about precisely how long your chapters should be but in action sequences they can generally run a little longer because your reader is probably going to be racing along through the scene, carried away by all the action.

Obviously your action sequence may well run much longer than one chapter, but it's perfectly okay to split them up into separate chapters. This also provides the perfect opportunity for more cliff–hangers, and that's where the *real* money is when it comes to writing an exciting action sequence.

They've done it! No they haven't! Yes, they have! Or have they?!

When it comes to action, just like in the movies, you want your reader right on the edge of their seat. Their heart should start thumping a little quicker, their muscles should tense up a little more and they should be rooting for your hero and cursing the enemy bearing down upon them.

To extract the maximum tension, excitement and suspense from your action scene, it should have the same structure as a full–length novel. There should be a hook, an inciting event, two turning points, a point of no return, a rug–pulling moment and a final climax.

Let's use an example in order to show how I would put it all together. Remember that this is something in which, within the scene, you can really play God. As long as the scene leads the protagonist and antagonist closer to their ultimate goals, anything is fair game as long as it is believable and enjoyable for the reader. I will write this in one go (I promise) basically making it up as I go to show how structure helps create a scene.

Scene premise: Barry and Sarah are fleeing Victor McVillain and his henchmen.

Location: In vehicles, across a jungle track in Indonesia.

Goal: Escape with the valuable and ancient artefact, a golden idol, from the tomb they've raided.

Hook: Barry and Sarah rush out from the tomb with their stolen artefact. They jump into their jeep and accelerate away.

Inciting Event: Victor McVillain and his men arrive in a heavily armed helicopter gunship and give chase. Victor uses a loud hailer to offer them freedom in return for the artefact.

Turning Point 1: Barry won't give up their prize and so the chase *really* heats up. Sally argues with him about this, generating conflict as she feels it's too dangerous to risk being shot by the gunship.

Point of No Return: The gunship attacks, firing bullets that hit the jeep and cause Barry to lose control. He and Sally hurl themselves out before the stricken jeep *skids off a cliff*! Barry and Sally are left dangling off the cliff edge, their transport lost.

Turning Point 2: Barry and Sally scramble back into the jungle and flee on foot but the helicopter cuts them off and lands, Victor's gunmen pouring into the jungle to hunt them down. Sally pleads for Barry to hand over the idol, but Barry won't do it and storms off.

Rug–pulling moment: Barry and Sally are split up in the dense jungle. Barry slips past the henchmen and makes for freedom, but then he hears Sally scream! She's been captured! (Worst possible thing to happen to him!) Barry sneaks back and hides in a bush as he sees the helicopter move in.

Climax: Victor's men hold Sally hostage as the helicopter hovers just over the clearing. Victor McVillain jumps out and uses the loud hailer to demand the idol.

Barry takes the idol in his hand and makes his decision… (A character defining moment – will he try to save Sally, or flee?)

I timed myself writing the above and it took me just over four minutes, plus a minute or so to edit and make small alterations. Think *freely*, let the momentum of the scene spark creativity. I only made two corrections and added the jeep skidding off a cliff instead of just hitting a tree because it added more action and tension. I then added Sally arguing about their course of action to introduce conflict into the scene before adding the line about the helicopter hovering *above* the clearing for reasons written below.

EXERCISE 6

What does Barry do to extricate both himself and Sally from their predicament? See if you can think of something that could both affect Barry's character development and cause chaos in the scene, perhaps enough that Sally could get free of her captors?
Two of my ideas would be;

1) Barry positions himself near the cliff and threatens to toss the idol over it if Sally is not freed. *Would Victor shrug and say: "Go ahead, we'll find it later!"?*
2) Barry hurls the idol into the helicopter's spinning blades, sacrificing it to give Sally a brief window of opportunity to flee as the henchmen scatter to avoid the lethal debris. *Highly risky, but it develops his character in terms of his relationship with Sally and this is an action scene after all…*

The important thing to remember is that the characters must go through the same increasing stakes, struggles and failures in your action scenes as they do throughout the whole novel. The more mini–climaxes and failures you can put into your scenes, the better your action sequences will become. It doesn't matter what a story is about, whether it's romance, thriller, slasher or sci–fi : conflict is what drives the reader's need to discover *what happens next*. Here's another one;

Bob has a problem – he owes £5,000 to Tom for a bet gone bad but he can't afford to pay.
Boring story hook, right?
The thing is, Tom's a violent drunkard and is also short of cash for his next drug fix. His first stop is going to be Bob's place of work – a bank.
A bit better.
Bob's stuck at work, and worse, his wife Mary runs the front desk. She'll see everything, and Tom always gets out of work at 3pm. Bob can't leave until 4pm.
The tension deepens as we move onto Turning Point One.
Bob knows that Tom will create a scene in the bank, and Bob's not a violent man. He's a bit of a coward actually but he loves his wife and doesn't want her to

worry or discover what's going on (create reader sympathy and empathy). He's got to get out of this, and in his desperation Bob decides that means only one thing: stealing cash from the bank's vault to pay off Tom. (The Point of No Return is when Bob decides on this course of action and plans how he'll do it – there's no going back now).

Much better. Now we need an *even better* crisis point because we need to escalate that tension, just because we can, right?!

But then Bob sees Tom across the street through the bank windows! He's off work early! Bob's now got half the time he thought he had to get the cash, and Mary's going to see Tom come into the bank. Tom's crossing the street outside, swaggering and clearly drunk, anger writ large across his features.

Bob makes for the vault and grabs handfuls of cash. He whirls... to see the bank manager staring at him in horror. The manager demands to know what he's doing and won't let Bob leave. Tom must be almost inside the bank! Bob has seconds to act! (The rug–pulling moment).

EXERCISE 7

Write the last notations for the scene. What would *you* have Bob do? He can't just come clean and admit his dilemma, because that's what law–abiding citizens like you and I would do. He is a character and thus he *must* do something that matches his desperation. Think freely, toss ideas out there no matter how ridiculous they may initially seem, because they may lead to something inspired.

I think maybe Bob punches the manager and makes to pay off Tom. But maybe Tom's holding the bank up to get the cash instead of threatening Bob, thus giving Bob a potential way out of things? Maybe Tom's taken Mary hostage? Maybe Mary's got a hold of the gun and has shot Tom (!).

You can play God, and you should endeavour wherever possible to ensure that not only does your character find themselves in a situation where it seems that they cannot possibly prevail or escape their predicament, but that they *do* find a way. The more innovative or unexpected their victory is, the more excited and inspired will be your readers.

Perhaps your hero Daisy is trapped in an alleyway and facing two sadistic killers. It seems that she cannot possibly defeat them. Yet, if you placed a subtle "plant" earlier in the novel that Daisy is a skilled martial artist, or always carries a gun, or is a talented athlete, then your action scene can have a suitably satisfying climax as Daisy suddenly fights her way out of the alley. Or, perhaps the alley is thin enough and her athletic prowess such that she climbs upward, her legs and arms pressing against the opposite walls so that she gets out of her assailant's reach and escapes?

Think *freely*, seek clever escapes and satisfying conclusions.

My point is, to create real tension in an action sequence doesn't require nations pointing nuclear warheads at each other. It requires only those two important things: opposing motivations of the characters concerned and an escalation of conflict over those opposed motivations – the great purpose and great stress. If you can, a third great addition is a sudden twist that alters the story path, catching the reader out.

Escalation of tension should occur not just in a scene but across an entire story, with the highest stakes and greatest risk coming in the final part of the story (or scene). Strong motivations will drive your characters to perform greater acts of risk in order to achieve their story goals, and create just the kind of tension in the process that you're looking for. The higher the stakes, the higher the tension or action and the deeper you can dig your characters into their pit of despair and desperation before their final rise to victory.

December 2012

It's hard to describe how difficult it is to deal with a sudden and dramatic change in fortune, when there are so many differing ways in which people adapt (or not) to adversity. For over a year I had been one of Simon & Schuster's Top 100 authors, a significant achievement and a rank that few writers manage to attain in their careers. But the sudden paradigm shift in publishing trends that emerged late in 2012 were ones that neither publishers nor authors could have predicted. In the wake of the economic crash of 2008 and the aftershocks that continued for many years afterward, new forms of publishing and new genre trends emerged that changed publishing forever. No industry, not even the mighty behemoth that was international publishing, could have withstood the triple blows that rained down upon it in 2011 and 2012.

The first impact was the one that occurred outside the publishing world: the economic crash of 2008 created mass redundancies across most western countries, foreclosures in the US, home repossessions in the UK, manufacturing decline and other economic disasters that would take years to overcome. All of that meant that many people had more on their minds than spending money on their favourite author's latest release.

The second impact was the shift in reader's habits, away from the action and adventure genre made successful for a decade by authors like Dan Brown, toward dark psychological tales by authors such as Gillian Flynn. Gone Girl, one of the biggest hits of the decade, set in motion a new genre that fed the statistic that 80% of all readers are female. Targeting a near–limitless supply of voracious readers, books like Gone Girl, The Shining Girls and The Girl on the Train shot to the tops of the charts one after another and swept all before them. Such are the vagaries of publishing, and trend shifts are common in the industry just as they are in movies and music: tastes change, and those who are unable to adapt to the changes tend to die off.

But perhaps the most long–term damage to the traditional publishing industry was caused by the sudden and meteoric rise of independent digital publishing, a new and exciting avenue driven largely by the growth of the on–line retail giant Amazon. In 2011, just as my debut Covenant was hitting the shelves for the first time, Amazon's Kindle Direct Publishing introduced readers to a new breed of superstar author: one who had no agent, no publisher, in fact no connection to the industry at all and yet was able to earn a living selling books across the globe through Amazon. With iBookstore, Kobo and others swiftly joining the race created by Amazon's release of its Kindle e–reader, the traditional publishing juggernaut was swiftly cut off from a massive chunk of the reading public.

In 2012, after handing in the fifth in my Ethan Warner series of books to my editor at Simon & Schuster, I learned that they would not be buying any further titles in the series. Game over. Despite having already sold over 100,000 copies my genre was no longer at the top of the game and publishing houses the world over were scrambling desperately to understand the new and unexpected digital competition. With no clear plan and no idea of what to do about the threat, publishers simply closed ranks, reduced lists, made redundancies and hunkered down to wait out the storm. Unless an author was in the very top branches of their sales tree or was willing to accept paltry advances for their books, they were effectively out of a job.

After fifteen years of effort I had signed my first major publishing deal in September 2010. Just two years later the dream was over.

XI: Give me a break….

Beats and pauses, breaks and troughs.

Even in the most action–packed, fast–paced roller–coaster of a thriller
there *must* be moments when the reader has time to reflect on what's happened and
draw conclusions of their own, especially if you're writing a crime novel. It's not
good for the reader to be so constantly on the edge of their seat that they can barely
breathe – it's exhausting and could even be detrimental to the book you're trying to
write. Not to mention the fact that if it was you who had just survived a violent car
chase and hand–to–hand fight for life with a deranged serial killer, you might need
a sit down and a cup of tea to take stock.

Rather like the "*talky*" bits in the movies, these chapters allow your reader to
assimilate what they've learned while also taking on new information about your
character's journey. Known as *breaks* or *troughs*, they constitute a chapter or two
between each of the big set–piece action scenes that you've created as you plotted
your novel. Such narrative and dialogue also allows for character development: a
simple example would be the chalk–and–cheese heroes who don't get along. After
a major action sequence in which one reluctantly saves the life of the other, the
dynamic between them would naturally alter and be portrayed in the trough
between set pieces. Mutual, if reluctant, respect might develop and a softening of
tone between them compared to the preceding chapters of your novel.

Then, if you're thinking out of the box, this could become an opportunity to
develop a major plot point later in the novel: perhaps the saving of the other's life
was a deliberate attempt to engender trust, when in fact the apparent hero is in fact
a villain… (Think freely, keep the potential *duality* of scenes in mind at all times,
just as I did when writing the preceding paragraph).

Information dumps.

Novice authors are often wary of these breaks and troughs and feel the need to
fill the voids with long and unnecessary explanations of a character's past history,
or perhaps extensive and detailed accounts of some pivotal fact to show how much
research they've done and how clever they are. I was once a victim of this trait
until I got the mantra *less is more* into my head.

Called information dumps, these are endless paragraphs of material spouted by characters who might otherwise not talk in such a way, or lengthy paragraphs of boring exposition. Avoid them at all costs. In my *Warner & Lopez* series the duo are often chasing some kind of technological gadgetry that could change the world, and because that McGuffin is usually based on something in the real world it's immensely tempting to rattle on for a page or two about how clever it all is. The problem with that is that it becomes boring unless the reader really is a tech–head.

My way of imparting information to the reader without droning on like a text book is to split the explanations up into a mixture of narrative, dialogue and cliff–hangers. *Cliff–hangers, in dialogue?* Damned straight, and why the hell not? If you have something interesting to say, extract the maximum amount of entertainment that you can from it and deliver that entertainment to your readers. Remember in a previous chapter how I spoke about characterization, about how I might give one character a sort of catch–phrase that suits them best? One of the examples I used was that of Doug Jarvis, who works for the Defense Intelligence Agency as the handler of Warner and Lopez in the series. He's usually the one who explains, at each novel's first Turning Point, what the unusual and impressive technological marvel it is that Warner and Lopez will be chasing. At a key point in the conversation, Ethan or Nicola will ask a question about the device / artefact, and Jarvis will reply;

'You'll have to see that to believe it.'

Here, the chapter typically ends on a cliff–hanger. The reader now wants to keep the pages turning to see *what* it is they'll have to *see* to *believe.*

Keep the conversation alive, keep the narrative short and sweet, draw from your research and your plot every last ounce of tension, excitement and conflict that you can even when nobody is firing a gun or chasing a criminal. Every little bit helps and keeps the reader on their toes waiting for the next unexpected event.

The coming storm

This method of keeping the reader engaged while in a trough in the story can keep them turning pages, but with pace in mind one should also consider the bigger story behind the scene. Even in the quietest moments of a story the reader should always be aware of the coming storm, the fact that this quiet spot is merely an interlude on the greater journey.

I often use narrative and dialogue, as described above, to keep this sense of the story alive but perhaps your story is a novel that cannot do this. I have such things as gadgetry and high–concept science to fall back on but a romance novel doesn't, and to some extent nor would a horror story or a children's book. Authors in these genres must focus more deeply on elements of character and plot in order to draw the greatest possible suspense from the story and keep the reader aware of the traumas their hero is yet to face.

Remember that even in these quietest of moments the story must always be marching onward toward the climax, the final confrontation between your protagonist and antagonist, and that every word spoken, every thought imparted and every location visited must be with that in mind. Anything else in there, no matter how much you like it, must be excised to avoid losing your reader between the larger set–piece scenes.

It is often during these breaks and troughs that a hero, or villain, will learn something unexpected, perhaps through their own investigative work or from a secondary character. These are great moments to introduce a twist in the story.

Twists and turns.

For me, creating unexpected twists in a story is one of the greatest pleasures of writing fiction. It's like playing God with the reader, deliberately coaxing them along into believing that X is going to happen, and just when they're least expecting it hitting them instead with a sledgehammer Y and blowing the hero's campaign out of the water.

For twists to work coherently generally requires the author to have done some elementary plotting first, or to have written a good portion of the story. Twists require *connections* and *conflict*, the essential ingredients for a character to be sufficiently motivated to do something completely unexpected or for conditions to be reached that a major revelation changes the course of the plot. Likewise, those plants and pay–offs mentioned earlier that maybe made no sense in the earlier sections of the story or were subtle enough to be noticed only subliminally by the reader suddenly take on new significance as the twist plays out and mysteries are resolved.

I often only come up with such twists and turns when I'm maybe half–way through a novel, and the differing threads of the story start to come together. Suddenly I can see opportunities for new twists developing as the story progresses, or a character written as a good–guy suddenly is positioned in such a way that I see the capacity for them to become a villain, or be exposed as one. Free thinking and duality help to conjure up these twists using the components of the story that are already in place.

Writing Tip

Do NOT just keep on writing when you have such ideas for major twists that change the course of your plot, convincing yourself that you'll remember the twist later. Like dreams, these ideas can slip away so easily and I guarantee that you'll be cursing yourself later if you forget them. Write them down the very moment you have them, even if it's only a couple of lines to jog your memory in days, weeks or even months' time when you come to do your edits. When you look back through these notes, you'll be overjoyed that you wrote them down and your first editorial pass on your manuscript will be all the better for it.

These moments of revelation are a joy in writing fiction just as much as reading them, and should be grasped whenever they come along. Thinking outside of the box, keeping an eye on both the individual chapter and the bigger picture is essential in being able to spot such opportunities in your writing. Keeping notes and having at *minimum* a loose plot in place increases your chances of picking up on these quirks of writing and twisting them whichever way you want. Then, when you edit your novel, you can head back into the chapters preceding the twist and drop in fresh, subtle hints (plants) to the reader of what is to come later. Obviously you have to be careful not to overdo it and telegraph to your reader the fact that Victor Villainous McVillain might possibly be a bad guy: usually just one or two tiny snippets of information buried somewhere in the narrative, or something mentioned in dialogue by one of the characters can provide the thread that leads to your big reveal. Your readers will gasp and wonder how on earth you could possibly have crafted such a cunning twist that they didn't see coming. It is this method by which so many crime authors both reveal and at the same time conceal the identity of the villain, their readers stunned when the revelation comes and wondering how on earth they didn't spot the signs in the story before that moment finally arrived.

The big twist usually either comes at Turning Point Two, the moment when your hero is almost at the point of victory and it seems that nothing can stop them now (and represents the rug–pulling moment), or at the very end of your tale when some previously unknown fact is revealed (the climax and denouement).

SPOILER ALERT: *The Sixth Sense*

A good example of a climatic twist is the movie *The Sixth Sense*, when it is finally revealed that Bruce Willis's character is in fact himself a ghost. But, did you notice the other plants and pay–offs throughout the movie? I didn't when I first watched it, but whenever the audience saw red on the screen a ghost would appear. Very subtle, but it was there. Nor did I see coming that devastating twist at the end but it entirely changed the movie and provoked Bruce's character to tie up the final loose threads of the story: saying goodbye to his troubled widow, leaving her to live her life in peace before making his own final journey, this time into an unknown afterlife that we do not see.

Don't think that just because twists can be fun that you absolutely *have* to get one into your novel somehow. Plenty of superb books, the majority in fact, survive perfectly well without them. However, minor twists and turns are essential in keeping your reader engaged and asking themselves questions about your characters and where the story is taking them. Did Barney *really* murder his wife or could somebody have *planted* the gun? Didn't one of the characters say that their neighbour once owned a *pistol*? Or was it the *gun shop* owner in the next town, who used to *date* Barney's *wife* at high school?

Build questions with mystery and plants and pay them off with satisfying conclusions. Use breaks and troughs to give your reader time to breathe, and then send your characters hurtling toward their goal with dramatic twists and turns and explosive set pieces.

When plotting and writing, look for anything that can enhance conflict and tension, mystery and flow. That scene that doesn't have much going on, just information flow for the reader? Throw some conflict in there to jazz it up, but make sure that the conflict you set up is paid–off later in the story. Don't leave readers hanging and always reach a satisfying conclusion to the conflict, even if it means that one of your characters suffers a tragic demise because of it. If they're the kind of character that just won't quit, then they should push on until it kills them. It takes *minutes* to dream up reasons for conflict in novels, because as the author you're playing God and can invent *anything* to drive your characters forward.

In summary, for all of the scenes in your novel consider the following seven factors at *all* times;

Mystery, flow, conflict, tension, suspense, motivation, character.

I'm half way through and my novel is crap!

Good, congratulations!

I don't think that I've ever met a novelist who doesn't feel this way about their latest book, no matter how many times they've been through the process or how many millions of copies they may have sold. You're in good company so don't worry about it.

I have heard many, many authors say that they've reached the half–way point in their novels and abandoned the work because it "just wasn't working".

This is without a doubt the worst thing that an author can do. Just because a novel isn't working *yet* does not mean it's not going to work *later*. I often feel the same about my own work and yet I push on because I have an understanding that when I have a completed draft before me, and when I've written out my Chapter Map so that I can see the whole picture instead of trying to assess an entire novel with my mind and memory alone, I will be able to see what's wrong and do something about it.

Your instincts that your half–written novel isn't yet up to scratch may well be correct, but it's a *half–written* novel! It isn't even finished yet! Complete the damned thing before you start tearing it apart. Words written are never really wasted, and the temptation to abandon a project and start on some new idea is often overwhelming, but *don't* do it! Plot and plan the new idea while you're working on the current one. Finish the job! Trust me, when you've got that completed first draft before you, a full–length novel that's ready for editing and polishing, your enthusiasm for the project will return in time because you've written a *whole novel*. I've lost count of the number of times I've published a novel that I felt like abandoning at one point or another, and watched it become the bestselling book I'd written yet.

You're not a good judge of your own work because, by definition, you're up to your neck in it. So, keep writing until you've finished your first full manuscript. Don't quit, no matter how long it takes or how many times you feel that your work's not up to scratch. Here's a quote from me that I often use when chatting to aspiring writers who feel that they'll never make it into a career as a full–time author.

"I didn't get through because I was the best. I got through because I learned never to quit."
Dean Crawford

May 2013

They say that necessity is the mother of invention.

After Simon & Schuster dropped the bombshell that novels in my Ethan Warner series would no longer be bought by them, I had a long chat or two with my agent and came up with a new plan. I'd had an idea for a post–apocalyptic novel based on something that actually happened in 1859, "The Carrington Event". A gigantic solar storm that blew up telegraph machines across the world, if such a storm were to strike the world today it would cripple modern society overnight. Luigi loved the idea and I spent the next five months writing the book, which I titled "Eden". When I finished the book I was extremely excited at its prospects but I was also somewhat uncertain of what to do with it.

I had spent a while watching the growth of independent publishing and I was starting to see that far from being either a flash–in–the–pan or something that "people who couldn't get published properly" did, independent digital publishing was a genuine and fast–growing means of reaching readers. Indie authors were releasing titles at prices which undercut their traditionally published competition, drawing readers away from the bookstores, and some authors were making tremendous sums of income, sufficient to put most traditionally published authors to shame.

I had a mortgage to pay, my wife had been made redundant, our daughter was growing in both stature and cost and I had to think fast. We had saved most of the money I'd made from my Simon & Schuster contracts but I didn't want to rest on my laurels. I had a decision to make, and during a family holiday in May 2013 after my book Eden had been sent by Luigi out to auction with publishers I intimated to my family that if Eden didn't sell, I might strike out on my own with it.

Just two years after first getting a publisher, I was thinking about ditching the industry altogether because I thought I might be able to do a better job myself.

XII: Editing

Now that you've reached the end of your novel, chances are that you'll feel somewhat unusual: elated that you've achieved something so remarkable and perhaps a little empty after so much hard work. It's also possible that you'll feel deflated, knowing in your heart of hearts that the novel is filled with errors or scenes that don't match. The huge amount of further work awaiting you might fill you with depression and a lack of motivation to continue any further.

Welcome to the world of editing.

Before you reach for the wine and drown your sorrows, I'd like to take a moment to let you in on a secret: it's the same for *every* single author in the world, no matter how perfect they may seem to be on the outside. Editing is always hard, whether it's done on the fly (by a few authors) or done at the end of the first draft (by the majority). Editing requires the same attention to detail as writing itself, and it often takes as long to successfully and competently edit your work as it did to write it in the first place.

Take heart, however, for it isn't *all* bad. For a start, you just wrote a novel so pat yourself on the back. Treat yourself to a drink. Secondly, you should know that from this moment on, every edit that you perform will make this novel of yours *better*. When every typo is corrected, every word of dialogue is sharpened and every line of prose is honed to perfection, editing can turn a mediocre book into a masterpiece.

To start with, give yourself a week or two off from your writing. Seriously, do it. Take a break. If you cannot leave writing alone, start planning or thinking about a new novel or begin research for it. The temptation to *strike while the iron's hot* and start editing the draft you've just finished will almost certainly be overwhelming but it won't help you much because you need time *away* from the manuscript to be able to judge it with any reasonable accuracy. Leave it alone, enjoy a rest and come back to your treasured novel ready to look at it with a fresh eye. Then, when you're ready and you've had some time away, sit down somewhere comfortable with your book. Have a notepad and pen handy for essential notes, but at this stage your job is just to read the damned thing.

It's crap, but it could be good.

This is not an unusual reaction to re–reading one's first novel. Having had a couple of weeks away you'll probably have read through and felt that some bits were good, some bits were bad and some bits need moving to preserve chronological timelines. You'll also likely find out that you wrote far more typos and made many more mistakes than you realised.

All normal stuff. What you need to do here is focus on the natural order of editing, which I perform in the following manner

1. Structural Edit
2. Line Edit.
3. Final edit.

Structural Edit

This is where you take a look at the overall novel and decide what chapters are in the wrong place, where new chapters need to be added and which others need to be removed, if any. This is the biggest of the edits in terms of the turmoil and confusion that can be caused, so it's absolutely essential that you start this process with a clear plan in mind. It doesn't matter whether you're a panster or a plotter when you're writing a first draft: now you have to be a true plotter or you'll be chasing your tail for months.

I'll say this in *Capitalese* so that you don't damned well forget it:

NEVER EDIT WITHOUT A PLAN

There, that told you.

In order to achieve that plan, I again use the same template I use when originally planning my novels: the Chapter Map. Overleaf is an image of the chapter map from my last novel (at the time of writing) *The Genesis Cypher*, created after finishing the first draft.

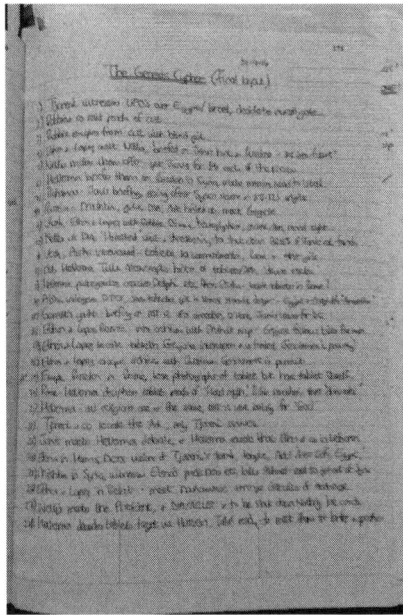

Just like the version I showed you earlier in the book there's nothing particularly complex about it, just the chapter number and a brief line about what happens within that chapter. Sometimes I will add questions at the end of the notations, or draw red arrows from a chapter I think needs moving to the location I think it would serve the story better. The image above only depicts one page but it actually ran to two, the book having 43 chapters in the first draft.

Having this *God's Eye* view of the novel helps me to keep track of that all–important bigger picture while at the same time making smaller adjustments in terms of individual chapters and scenes. It also ensures that if I *do* move a chapter, I can see how that move affects what characters know at any given point in the story, an important factor in maintaining continuity. A book doesn't read well if you have a character in two places at once, for instance, or a pregnancy that lasts eighteen months. Having a chapter map to scrutinize those details quickly and easily covers you against such flaws. (Again, for those authors who prefer to use digital plotting programs like *Scrivener* the same rules apply, it's only the medium that is different).

What you're looking for is that all–important *flow*. Each chapter should flow into the next both logically and chronologically. The reader should never learn about something earlier than the main characters, unless of course you're using that method as a means to create tension in the story: i.e, the reader is *shown* (not told!) that Bill and Mary are being spied upon by a third party, but the characters themselves don't know it yet.

I often have to write out my chapter map two or three times when going through the structural edit, scrolling through my novel for each chapter and writing a single line notation as to the contents of those chapters before reviewing them again and making more changes. Most times, this involves adding a new chapter or a new scene because I've seen opportunities for new story threads that are exciting or interesting, or places for cliff–hangers that I hadn't spotted before. Remember the layout of your three–act structure, and the increasing levels of tension as the novel progresses:

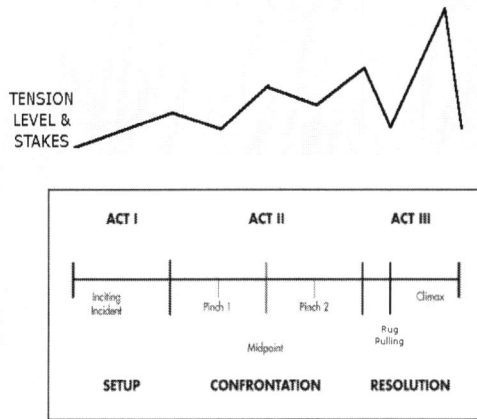

Cliff–hangers.

These are always good, and as discussed in previous chapters I use them a lot in different forms. Ending a chapter at a crucial moment is one of the most often used techniques to get your reader to think: "go on then, I'll just read *one more* chapter to see what happens next." Reading one more chapter or one more page is precisely what you want your readers to be doing, so placing your hero or heroine in a life–threatening situation at the end of a chapter is a brilliant way of doing this. Be careful, however, and remember that the reader needs a rest from time to time: an endless series of cliff–hangers is going to get tiresome pretty quickly and it's easy to overplay your hand.

Some readers don't like to be left on the cliff too long, either. So, if your hero is dangling from the end of a tall crane with one hand and their fingers are slipping as they reach the end of the chapter, it's not always a great idea to leave them there while you explore another character's story for a couple of chapters before returning to your imperilled hero. Allow them to escape their predicament before moving on to other story threads. However, if your valiant hero Jared is about to enter a dangerous building filled with criminals that he or she must engage and defeat in battle, then just as they burst in you could move on for a single chapter to another scene, keeping your reader on tenterhooks about what's going to happen to Jared next.

I often use this technique by having two characters, separated by great distances but connected by the fact that what happens to one will directly affect the other. Below is a hypothetical scene from my *Warner & Lopez* series of how this process might break down either as individual scenes within a chapter or individual chapters:

Scene i) Doug Jarvis is in Washington DC, overseeing a DIA mission to attack a terrorist compound in Somalia where hostages are being held. The DIA is under pressure as Homeland believe the crucial operation to be illegal and want to shut it down.

Scene ii) At the site of the attack in Somalia, Ethan and Nicola are closing in on the compound. *Tension.* Ethan and Nicola lead the charge and engage in a gun battle with the brutal terrorists. They're getting the upper hand when suddenly enemy reinforcements rush in from nearby, forcing Ethan to call in air support. *Action / cliff hanger.*

Scene iii) Doug is about to make the call for air support when Homeland burst into the building and disrupt the operation! An argument ensues as Homeland try to shut the covert operation down. *Conflict / tension / cliff hanger.*

Scene iv) Ethan and Nicola are cornered under heavy fire and are on the verge of being caught! More enemy come plunging into the compound, all firing at once! They've killed many of the enemy soldier's friends, so now the Somalians' blood is up – Ethan and Nicola won't get out alive if they're caught!

Scene v) Doug and his team are arrested, but did they get the command for the air support off in time and did it get through to the air support? The reader isn't informed, so they don't know what's going to happen! *Tension / cliff hanger.*

Scene vi) Ethan and Nicola are surrounded and defeated (*rug–pulling moment*)! They drop their weapons and put up their hands. The vicious leader of the Somalian gang confronts them and draws a huge, bloodied blade. He throws his arm back to hack them to death…. *Cliff–hanger*

… when gunfire rips through him and his men as Apache attack helicopters swoop in to rescue Ethan and Nicola from certain death. The hostages are freed and the day is saved at the last moment.

This is a simple example but once again you get the idea: escalating tension and ever–higher stakes, followed by a rug–pulling moment, a twist and a satisfying climax and conclusion. Draw your reader along for as long as you can, stretch out those moments of tension, *make them wait* for as long as you possibly can! The more you draw from each scene, the more exciting those scenes will be, just remember that the pay–off must make sense and the action must be interspersed with lulls and troughs to give the reader, and your intrepid heroes, a break.

Observe your manuscript and ensure that the general flow of the work moves logically and smoothly from action sequences to breaks and troughs, with the stakes being raised ever higher as the story progresses. Bridging scenes and extra paragraphs here and there may be required to achieve this, and it is a wise author who makes themselves an *editing list*.

This is a chronological series of editing tasks working from the front of the book to the back that you can tick off one by one as you complete them. Mine usually consist of no more than a chapter number and a brief line or two about what I need to write or alter to make a proper plant / pay–off / character development or whatever. No matter how long the list becomes, as you work through them and tick them off you know that your novel is gradually improving with each completed task. Such a list can also be a handy psychological boost too, as you see your progress and have a visual idea of how much better your work is becoming as the editing continues.

Line edit.

Once you're happy with the overall structure of your novel, it's time to look at the detail. This means reading through the entire book again from the first page to the last, examining each and every line in the search for a number of things: *typos, over–writing, telling–not–showing, poor prose, and the presence of sufficient flow, mystery, conflict, tension, character and suspense as required by the scenes in question.*

During the line edit you should slowly move through your novel a line at a time, changing weak or passive words for better and more active alternatives, removing unnecessary adverbs, sharpening dialogue and prose. Take your time here. Make the effort to think for a moment about each chapter before you read it and assess what its purpose is and what the conclusion should be. If a word is not required, remove it no matter how great you think it might be. *Kill your darlings.* Or if you really like them just move them to somewhere they better belong.

Although viewed by some authors as a bit of a drag (me included!) this process is essential in polishing the work and taking your labour of love to the next level. Time spent here can really create something special, a final draft that takes full advantage of all of the ideas and scenes and characters that you've built up and creates a *true* blockbuster. I often pore over individual passages for ages, trying to imagine how it will be for a reader to encounter them for the first time, and ask myself a lot of questions;

Does that description really convey the scene well enough?
Does that line of dialogue really match the character speaking it? Could it be altered to better sound like them?
Is there enough suspense or conflict or action in the scene and is it believable?
That's a lovely bit of prose, but does it truly belong here? If not, can I put it somewhere else so it fits better?

Refer back to previous chapters in this book for examples that will help you in this line edit. Go through your novel one line at a time and really put in the effort required to tidy up every single word. Believe me, not a moment of this time will ever be wasted.

Final edit.

Yes, if you want to be truly thorough then there's *another* edit required. How you choose to do this one is up to you, but one of the most helpful things that you can do is to convert your novel into a different format for this final read–through.

The wonders of digital formatting mean that I now convert my novel at this point to HTML and load it onto my Kindle as a *.mobi* file. This means that I'm reading the book just as many of my readers will do, and thus both gives me a reader's perspective of my work and also makes it far, far easier to spot typos and other grammatical mistakes. After weeks or perhaps months of working on your book on a laptop, finally viewing it as a fully printed book or on a e–reader's screen really alters the appearance and helps your brain spot things it might otherwise have learned to gloss over.

A great guide to converting your work into Kindle format can be found here;

http://guidohenkel.com/2010/12/take-pride-in-your-ebook-formatting/

You'll need the free Notepad++ to convert the book to HTML format, found here:

https://notepad-plus-plus.org/

I then use the free *Calibre* software to convert the HTML into Kindle's .mobi format;

https://calibre-ebook.com/

Both are hugely reliable and I've used them for some twenty e–books without a fault. The first time you convert your book to Kindle is a time–consuming process, but once you've learned the ropes it can be done in very little time at all. (I can convert a book with basic formatting in twenty minutes, and in one hour with full formatting for a published book, so you'll soon learn how to do it). Make the effort to learn the process and you'll save a fortune for what is really a very simple task. Converting your own books will also come in extremely handy should you decide on a career as an independent author, dealt with in a later chapter.

Once you have your book ready, be it printed on paper or on your Kindle, settle down with your notepad and pen and start reading once again. Remember to note the location of any last remaining errors so that they can be found easily and corrected. Some authors like to mark the actual document in red pen, editor style, but if you're reading the book on your Kindle then just write a couple of words from the flawed passage down (or the typo) and the chapter number and you'll be able to find it easily later to correct it using the "*Search*" function in Notepad.

DO NOT skip this final read–through. Despite having written more than twenty novels, this part of the process still picks up an average of a hundred or so corrections for me. They might not be errors *per se*, but they can be lines of dialogue that still don't quite ring true, grammatical errors, lines of narrative where a word or two being swapped around would read better and so on.

Reading through your book for perhaps the third or fourth time is a tough call but trust me, it pays handsome dividends because when you're done with the final list of corrections (and you *will* find some!) you'll know that the final document is as good as you can make it on your own.

When you've finished the corrections, you can do two important things:

1) Relax, you've finally completed your novel.
2) Prepare to send it out for critical opinions from people you trust!

Lend me a hand..?

Sending your treasured manuscript out for other people to read is often a difficult task for authors. One of the hardest things to do is to accept criticism, especially on a piece of work that may have taken you months or even years to write. But accepting (sensible, constructive) criticism is one of the most important parts of being a professional author.

Choose two or three friends whose opinions you trust and who read in the genre you're writing in. This is important: don't send your action–adventure novel to somebody who normally reads weepy romance, as you're not going to get the enthusiasm you need in their feedback. They'll feel that reading such a book will be a slog for them, and if it's a real chore they'll probably not offer much detail in their response.

Hopefully, your chosen friends will jump at the chance to check out your book. If you're in a writing circle or a member of a book club, even better. Make sure to tell your friends that you're steeled for *honest*, critical feedback. If they don't like the book then they should say so, but it's extremely important that they should also say *why* they didn't like it.

We all want to think that everybody will love our work, but in truth there is a small clique of readers who will think it's the best thing since *Gone with the Wind* and they'll be clamouring for a sequel. Fortunately for authors, that small clique when scaled up to the size of the general reading public can mean that literally millions of people may like your book, but for now it's down to two or three friends to let you know their opinion.

Many long days and nights of anxiety will follow as you await the verdict. Try not to get too riled up and just wait it out. If you've done a professional job then it should be a given that your friends won't burn their copy of the book and refuse to ever speak to you again. If they didn't like it, it'll not be because it's full of typos or illiterate or a chronological mess: it'll be because they just didn't like some aspect of the story or perhaps one of the characters. Those kinds of things can be changed, but if you don't get the feedback you won't truly know what's working and what isn't.

Gary loved it but Catherine hated it. Now what do I do?

This is surprisingly common and it's all about taste. Let's say that two of your friends like the book but a third disliked it. Now is not the time to collapse in floods of agonised tears and demand of them how they *could be so callous?!* Ask all of them round one evening, fix them a drink and collect feedback from them all. Ask them what they *did* like as well as what they *didn't* and have as lively a discussion as you can about it. Find out what it is that makes some parts of your novel tick with perfect precision and others clunk along unconvincingly. Get a real feel for the feedback you're receiving and note it all down so that you can go away and make any changes you feel are necessary to give that final polish to your book. Doing it with friends and keeping everything in the open will help, trust me, in getting the clearest perspective of what needs altering in the book.

If one person hated a particular scene or character and another loved it, then it doesn't mean that they're both right or wrong. Changing scenes or characters depending on what critics say is a tough call for the author, and one has to remain clear–minded about just *how much* to change to appease those critics. The best compromise is to make every effort to smooth out any issues that *all* of your critics point out: perhaps a character they *all* detested, who wasn't a villain, or a scene that they *all* disliked or felt unconvincing because of a, b or c. However, for more uncertain criticisms where opinions conflict between readers, it's wise to only make *slight* changes if you can identify flaws that reduce the issues your friends have brought up. If authors edited based on the opinions of all our critics and reviewers, we would never release a title because the editing would never end, so be measured in your responses and have a good think about the feedback before making any final edits.

Don't get caught up in an endless loop of editing and re–editing. If you've got this far, then you should be at a stage where you're merely refining areas of the novel that didn't quite hit the spot with your critics. Only make a major change if *everybody* thought something or someone in the book was truly atrocious, because if they all thought that then it's likely that literary agents, publishers and the wider reading public will think the same and your treasured novel will be in danger of sinking before it's even got going. That's hugely important because once you've done these last revisions, out into the wider world is precisely where your novel is going next. Take your time and get it right so that you don't have to go through the drama of doing it all again.

June 2013

In May 2013 the last of the publishers Luigi had approached with "Eden", Ballantyne Books, got back to us and declined to offer, as had all of the publishers we approached. I won't pretend that I wasn't disappointed: it would have been nice to have secured another advance for two or three books that would have seen my family and I through a few more years, but by then even a contract wasn't a guarantee. The growing confusion and desperation of the traditional publishing world in the wake of the digital revolution had resulted in authors being chopped after their first books bombed, contacts annulled or even outright ignored, policies that would have been illegal in any other business but were now almost considered "normal" in publishing. At the same time I was meeting authors at a popular crime festival in the UK and hearing tales of woe, many previously successful full–time authors being forced back into day jobs because they couldn't make ends meet any more or had seen their contracts summarily axed.

Luigi was hugely apologetic and said that he couldn't understand why Eden hadn't got a publisher. Privately we knew that the editors had loved the book but the marketing teams at publishing houses had seen the changing trends in publishing and wanted to spend company money on "Gone Girl" clones, not male–led action adventure novels.

With no other option for Eden available, Luigi and I met for lunch and discussed the possibility of me writing books that might appeal to publishers keen to follow current trends. I agreed to start work on something that fit the bill, but I had also already made up my mind: Eden was going independent. When I suggested this to Luigi, he asked how anybody could possibly make money from a book that would cost less than a cup of coffee? That was the response I got from most in the industry. What the hell are you doing, Crawford? You're successfully traditionally published, even (a little bit) famous. Why would you willingly choose to enter the unsavoury bowels of self–publishing? How could you?

The more people said it was a bad idea, the more I began to think that they were more concerned about their own careers and the industry itself than whether independent publishing was actually a bad idea in business terms. I got hold of a copy of my sales from Simon & Schuster and studied the royalty reports. For every paperback I sold, I received 12% royalties on the net price, which worked out at approximately £0.25 before taxes. I then looked at Amazon's KDP program and saw that authors got 70% royalty on the net price, which at that time for a book being sold for £2.99 meant about £2.10 per book before taxes, and that was after Amazon had taken their thirty per cent.

I then conducted a very swift and un–scientific calculation on the back of an envelope. If I sold just 50 books per day on Amazon worldwide, that would be equivalent to about £105 per day in earnings. I did another little sum and then sat back and stared at the calculator in amazement. Selling just fifty books per day on Amazon across the whole world would earn me £38,325 per year. The average author in the UK earns very much less than £10,000 per year, and they have to sell the rights to their work for up to 35 years for the privilege, and then usually have to do all their own advertising and marketing anyway.

I decided that there was no longer any reason not to try. Just because female–orientated psychological fiction was selling in bookshops didn't mean that countless millions of male–led action adventure fans had spontaneously combusted overnight: the readers still had to be out there somewhere. I designed a cover for Eden and spent two weeks learning how to code HTML so that I could create a better interior layout than Amazon's standard design. I then spent a few days designed a logo for my company, Fictum Ltd, and attached it to the front of the e–book.

On July 23rd, 2013, I self–published Eden on Amazon's KDP and crossed my fingers. I hoped that the book would be a starting point and that it might earn me enough for some beer money each month. In truth, knowing by now how tough publishing of any kind could be, I didn't expect the novel to get very far and certainly not to rise up to the giddy heights that some Indie authors were now achieving in the USA and UK.

How little did I know…

PART 2: Your choices as an author.

Having crafted your masterpiece, it is now time to decide which route to take with it as you embark on your journey of publication. Although it may not feel like it, this is without a doubt one of the best times in history to become an author because publishing is no longer a one–horse race.

The rise of independent publishing via Amazon and other vendors has given a voice to countless thousands of authors who previously were deemed by publishers "unworthy" of a publishing contract, or simply were writing the wrong book at the wrong time. Until around 2011, if you wanted to buy a book you were largely restricted to what was on the shelves of your local bookstore or library. If they didn't have in stock something you fancied, then you just had to make do.

That time is over.

A reader has access to virtually any book they choose. Independent publishing ignores the whims of publishers and what they deem to be "hot" and thus publishable trends. Genres selling poorly in bookshops sell in droves in digital form and the figures prove it: over half of all e–books sold in the United States are now independently published. Indie authors out–sell all of the five major publishing houses *combined*. Just think about that for a moment. At the time of writing, in just five years since the Kindle e–reader was released independent publishing has taken more than a 50% share of the digital publishing market. Competitive pricing, quality editing, good cover art and solid writing have propelled to considerable fame and fortune authors who have never set foot in a publishing house or literary agent's office.

None the less, for many authors the idea of going it alone can be a formidable obstacle. The independent author is responsible not just for writing their books but for all editing, cover art, marketing, business decisions and much more. For this reason, the second part of this book will cover the details, advantages and pitfalls of both publishing methods. As an author who has experienced success on both sides of the publishing divide, I'm something of a rarity (at the time of writing, anyway) in that I have seen in depth how both the industry and Indie publishers work. This makes me what is known as a "hybrid author", sitting on the fence between both worlds and attempting to make the best of them. Insights that I've had can help you to decide which route is the best for you, or perhaps that whereas one of your books might be perfect for independent publishing, another might sit better with a traditional publisher.

To begin with we'll deal with the traditional route: how best to approach literary agents and thus publishers, and what to expect when a deal is struck and afterward, when your book hits the shelves for the first time. Then, we'll explore the world of independent publishing, the tools you'll need to succeed and what can await the author valiant enough to strike out on their own.

It should be emphasised again that *neither* route is easy. Both are littered with a small handful of superstars, behind which are countless hundreds of thousands of also–rans. The differences in what that means for author income and the chances of making a living as an author will be revealed, and I hope that by the end you will have a clearer idea of which route is the best for you.

XIII: "Please sir, may I have some more..?" Approaching literary agents

So you've decided to attempt the unenviable task of approaching a professional literary agency, in the hopes that they will love your work and guide you on the difficult journey toward a publishing deal with a major house.

Don't bother approaching publishers directly. Most won't accept unsolicited submissions these days and even if they do, by default the debut novelist is somewhat handicapped without an industry expert by their side to negotiate a fair deal. You need an agent to look after you, at least for a while, and it's there that you should begin the next stage of your journey.

The first step you should undertake is to obtain the details of all major literary agencies that handle the genre you're writing in. *DO NOT* approach anybody with your lovingly crafted romance if they only handle thrillers – all you'll be doing is wasting your time and everybody else's too. Take the time to do your research here: find the right kind of agents, who handle the right kind of material (from your perspective) and who are currently open to submissions. Virtually all respectable literary agents have websites detailing how they like to be approached: follow the instructions to the letter, *literally*. Remember, you're looking for ways to remove obstacles on your mission to publication. If an agent says don't staple the pages of your manuscript together, then don't. If they say they prefer e–mail submissions to paper then conform to their preferences. If they say they charge a "reading fee" then delete them from your list without hesitation. No reputable agent should charge a reading fee and you should be suspicious of any that do. They're there to make money as commission from publishing deals and royalties they achieve on your behalf, not grab cash before they've lifted a finger to help you.

On the subject of demands, many agencies will insist that they be approached exclusively by new authors. This is impractical for the simple reason that it often takes weeks, if not months, for an agency to get back to an author. My own literary agent, Luigi Bonomi of LBA Books in London, receives hundreds of submissions *per week*, thousands per year. LBA Books may take on one or two new clients from that formidable list each year. My advice is to select the best ten agents from your list and fire your submissions off one at a time every few days:

that ensures that the agencies in question at least have the chance to be "first come, first served" if your manuscript is truly stellar.

There's an awful lot of advice on the Internet about approach letters, synopsis packages and so on. Unfortunately much of it is contradictory and leaves the hopeful writer confused and uncertain about how to construct their approach.

I decided that the most important thing to consider was that agents are all very BUSY. They don't have much time to dedicate to searching through the 'slush–pile' and thus if something doesn't grab them within a few lines, they'll pass and move on. For this reason, my approach was as follows;

A) A *one–page* introductory letter.
B) A *one–page* synopsis, single line spaced.
C) The first three chapters (in my case, 21 pages in total).

All but the synopsis should be double spaced, 12 point Times New Roman just like this book, unless the agent specifies otherwise.

Below is my covering letter. This package was sent to ten of the top London literary agencies over a period of about two months. Of those ten, only two asked for the full manuscript. Of those, LBA signed me as a client and I turned down the other one shortly after (an odd experience in itself after many years of rejections!).

My advice is: be brief, exciting and *professional*. Not an easy combination – my letter took several days to perfect, but the effort was worth it in the end.

Dear Mr Bonomi,

What is the meaning of life? Where do we come from? What happens to us when we die?

I am writing to you as a novelist in search of representation for my commercial fiction thriller 'Genesis' (150,000 words). I understand that your client list includes the authors James Becker, David Gibbins and Matt Hilton, and believe that my work may be of interest to you. Genesis tells of a race–against–time search for the existence of ancient aliens, set against the political turmoil of the Middle East. As science discovers an extinct species of humanoid and destroys the notion of man as a special creation, powerful groups seek to destroy the evidence before humanity learns of its true origins.

I am thirty–seven years–old and have been writing for ten years, with previous work considered as full manuscripts by literary agents in 2007 (Lorella Belli and Sheil Land Associates). Genesis is the first in a planned series of novels featuring the protagonist Ethan Warner, a man with a talent for finding lost souls and exposing conspiracies in the world's most dangerous places.

I have enclosed the first three chapters of Genesis and a short synopsis as advised on your website. Many thanks in advance for any time spent considering my work.

Yours faithfully,

Mr Dean Crawford

That's it. Simple, no? Take note, however, of a few neat little tricks I used.

The "hook" in the first line of the letter, designed to grab the agent in question's attention by directly asking them the same question the book asks the reader; the mention of authors already on Luigi's client list who write books similar to mine, meaning that he may be interested in me as a potential new client; the fact that other reputable literary agents had gone as far as reading full manuscripts of mine after initial approaches, meaning that Luigi could take me seriously and the time likely wouldn't be wasted.

All of these, if you can include them, help to tell the agent that you're a serious writer and that you've taken the time to check out the agent's website and submission criteria. If you have any history of contact with literary agents that led to more than an immediate rejection it also tells them you're persistent and probably have a chance at success. Don't worry if those prior agents turned you down – virtually every agent in the business will have turned down a bestseller in their career. It took J.K. Rowling's literary agent over a year to sell *Harry Potter and the Philosopher's Stone* so don't worry, no good agent will worry much about previous rejections and will, if they like the sound of your story, start reading the chapters you've sent them to see if they live up to the promise of the submission letter.

The other side: My first meeting with a literary agent.

Be prepared for rejection. *A LOT* of rejection. I collected over one hundred rejections in the fifteen years I was writing novels before getting picked up. There's no need for you to go through all of that however. If your book is commercial and relevant and you're approaching agents professionally right from the get–go, then you're going to get some interest much quicker than I did.

Many rejections are made not because the book is bad or unprofessional, but because publishers just may not be looking for those kinds of books and agents know it. They're not going to waste time trying to sell a book that editors aren't looking for, much like you shouldn't expect a response from agents who don't represent the kind of material you're writing. Agents just don't have the time to write a critique of every submission they receive, so they generally send them back with a rejection slip and that's that.

Get used to it. You will be rejected, probably more than once, likely many times. Perseverance is your strongest ally in the fight to get past the other 99 per cent of authors and receive a request for the full manuscript to be sent to the agent in question. It might take weeks, months or even years, but if you're professional and determined and have a good book behind you, eventually it *will* happen.

"Reading a new submission is always a balancing act of differing emotions – is it well written? Does the plot work? Is the plot original enough to stand out? Do I

personally like it? Will editors also like it as much as I do? Are my instincts right on this one? All of these emotions go round and round your head as you are reading the manuscript but sometimes something you read leaps out at you from the very first page (and it is often from that first page) that makes your heart beat super–fast. Just read the first page of Dean Crawford's 'Covenant' and you will know what I mean. A couple of years back I picked up a mss that had been sent to me and started reading it on the way home. The first line began: "Sometimes Jonah Miller hated talking to the dead". As I read it on the train home, I couldn't stop reading and felt my heart beating faster and faster, it was such a gripping read. As I got off the train around 40 mins later, I was convinced that another agent might get to this before I did and I rang the author from the train platform, told him I loved what he had written and said I would love to represent him. A few months later I sold his novel to both a UK and US publisher and got a film option on it too. The feeling of excitement, and exhilaration, the rush to the head when reading something new and exciting is like nothing else. It's like a hit that you become addicted to and it is what keeps us going day in day out."

Luigi Bonomi, LBA Books

How long should I keep submitting the same book?

Before digital publishing became a "thing" I would have said forever, because what doesn't sell one year might well be in vogue the next. Keep an eye on bookshelves and the e–book charts, keep your ear to the ground if you can in the industry and find out what editors and agents are looking for. If your book's genre is suddenly hot, send those submission packages out again.

The same advice applies today, but with independent publishing you do have another option if all available literary agencies have been exhausted. This form of publishing is dealt with later in the book but, for now, if you've been submitting to agents for a year and haven't received a request for a full manuscript it's probably time to give Indie publishing a shot and earn some money from your book. Publishing a book independently doesn't rule you out of a traditional contract later, and in some cases success as an Indie title can attract publishers due to visibility in the charts.

In the interests of optimism, we'll continue on assuming that somewhere down the line an agent has expressed interest in your work.

Obviously my letter was successful, but it took a month to hear from LBA Books so be patient once your submission has been sent. My literary agent, Luigi Bonomi, likes to "check people out" a bit by suggesting radical re–writes to manuscripts in order to see if the potential client is willing to be professional and work hard to obtain their goals. I was willing to do whatever he suggested to make my novel *Genesis* a winner, and that professionalism won me an invite to the LBA offices in London. I was later to learn that Luigi had often turned down promising manuscripts because an author was unwilling to alter their work or seemed unprofessional in their approach to the industry. Remember that you as the author are approaching the agent, not the other way around.

Is this the right agent for me?

Having met a literary agent who is interested in your work, it can be tempting to sign up right away. However I would advise you that if you have any doubts at all about the agent you've met, you should think twice. This isn't just in terms of whether they're a reputable agent or not – you should *only* be approaching reputable agents who are members of an accredited association and who do not charge reading fees. What also matters is whether you get on well. Can you work with this person in the future? Do your ideas and hopes and expectations gel? I was very lucky in that Luigi and the entire team at LBA Books are renowned for being one of the most professional, friendly and successful agencies in the United Kingdom. Others, frankly, are not so lucky and there are as many horror stories of difficult agents as there are of difficult authors.

Pick wisely, take your time, get it right the first time and you'll be in safe hands. If in doubt, stay out, no matter how tempting it might be to sign on the dotted line. If you managed to get one reputable agent interested, you can manage another if things don't feel right for you.

Getting a contract.

Having been happily signed up to an agency, your agent will likely require some edits on your manuscript. Perform these as requested, let your agent's experience guide you in order to shape your novel into something that your agent knows will sell more easily to publishing houses. Sometimes (as in my case) this may require quite extensive editorial work, sometimes involving an editor hired by the agency in question.

Don't worry if this is the case, it's normal procedure. Your agent wants the book in absolute tip–top condition before it's sent out to publishers. They may have one or two specific editors in mind whom they know are looking for something just like your book, and that also means your book may find itself in competition with one or two others to win the prize of a publication deal. You're no longer writing alone now, however, and new eyes on your work can really make the difference when it comes to auction time.

The agent's submission.

When your agent feels that the manuscript is ready, he or she will write a submission letter much as you did when approaching agents. In this letter the agent will sell as best they can your work and set a date by which publishers should reply with a decision on whether they would like to offer for the publishing rights, before sending the full manuscript off to as many publishers as they think will be interested in acquiring the novel.

At each publisher approached, the editor will then read the manuscript and make a decision on whether or not they feel strongly enough about the material to fight for it. Yes, you read that right: *fight* for it.

In a publishing house it's not always the editors anymore who make the decision on what gets bought and when. The power of an editor to champion a title has diminished tremendously in the last twenty years. There are now marketing teams in publishing houses who scour the bookshops and sales figures of the land, deciding what's hot and what's not and how that should affect what editors can and cannot buy. If the editor in question likes your manuscript, they will bring it with them to their publisher's weekly acquisition meeting, where they will stand up in front of the Marketing and PR Departments and pitch your book. Other editors will be doing the same thing with other books that they have been sent by other agents, and still other editors at *other* publishing houses will be doing the same with both your book and *other* books.

After a period of mysterious contemplation, discussion and theorizing, the PR and Marketing Departments will make a decision on which of the pitched books the publisher will offer for, and also a budget beyond which they may not bid without further consultation. Amid this black art of corporate purchasing decisions, hopefully your manuscript will be chosen due to the editor *loving* it with all their heart and convincing everybody else they work with that it's *the one* for the publisher.

Yes, getting a literary agent on your side was only step one of the torturous process of getting published. Hopefully your agent will get calls or e–mails from a number of editors expressing an interest in your book and making an initial offer. Here is where things get a bit interesting…

A title auction.

If you're super lucky and two or three editors find themselves in competition for your book, a blind auction begins. This is where your talented and determined agent will attempt to play one publisher off another, pushing the advance for your books as high as they possibly dare before accepting the best offer.

If that offer is right, and if your agent and you are happy with it, then the offer will be accepted and it's time to crack open the champagne, because against all odds you've made it and suddenly you're a professional author with a true publishing contract!

Congratulations!

What is the purpose of all this? How and when do I get paid?

What happens is that publishers are presented with your novel and asked to pay an "advance" to the author up–front. The general idea is that the author gets paid some money before publication, and with most deals being for two or three books it commits the author to a contract with the publisher. The advance is then broken down into "tranches", usually in the following manner (for a hypothetical three–book deal).

Tranche 1) One payment for each book in the contract, upon signature.
Tranche 2) One payment per each delivered manuscript.
Tranche 3) One payment for each book upon its publication.

Thus, if an author was offered £9,000 pounds for three books, they would receive that advance in tranches of an initial payment £3,000, followed by payments of £1,000 for every completed manuscript delivered and £1,000 for each book published.

Most initial deals usually are for home country rights (USA rights in America, UK and Commonwealth in the United Kingdom and so on) but often a book will later be sold in multiple territories for translation. These deals also garner the author advances, the size of which depend on the size of the market the book is being sold into and to some extent how much was paid in the original deal and how much of a "buzz" was generated around that original acquisition. Agents will often attend major book fairs, such as London or Frankfurt, and sell titles there for foreign rights deals. If a major buzz has occurred around a UK and Commonwealth deal or a USA deal, the foreign publishers might flock to the title and further auctions may occur.

It all sounds fabulous, doesn't it?

The issue here is that, once sold, a book has to "earn out" it's advance before the author receives any further payments. That is, if the publisher spends £20,000 on a new author's first three books, then those books must sell at least £20,000 worth of copies before royalties are paid per copy sold to the author. One must remember that royalties are paid as a percentage of the net price: thus, a paperback might sell for £6.99, but the retailer might pay the publisher £2.99 per copy, and it is that value from which the author's royalty derives. Hence, on this example, the author will earn the princely sum of approximately £0.36 per copy sold.

Royalties are also paid on a sort of sliding scale outlined in a contract: the more books an author sells, the higher percentage of royalty they are paid, up to a maximum limit of perhaps 15 per cent. In addition your agent may sell foreign rights for translation in other countries, and these overseas sales typically return a greater royalty payment to the author than homeland sales. Overseas advances most usually pay the author eighty per cent, with the other twenty per cent or so going to the agent who negotiates the deal. However, it should be remembered that these sums all will be counted against your original advance, so the author still doesn't earn extra money until the home territory publisher's original costs are met.

The issue here is that the vast majority of published books fail to earn out the author's advance, and thus a lot of authors are living from advance deal to advance deal, contract to contract, and never sure of whether a publisher will buy their next book.

This, then, is the author's dilemma. A publisher might make a tremendous offer of a huge advance for a novel or series of novels, but such events are becoming increasingly rare for authors and literary agents alike as the industry contracts further in the wake of digital publishing. Although such major advances can change an author's life (they did mine) those books then have to earn back that huge advance before they represent a means of earning a *regular* income for authors. Conversely, an author might receive a small advance but then suddenly find themselves with a genuine bestseller on their hands and earn vast amounts of money (ask J.K Rowling about that wonderful eventuality).

Your circumstances as an author, and the guidance you should receive from your literary agent, will help you to decide which offers to take and which to reject should the time come that your book is under offer.

December 2013

Blockbuster.

I couldn't have predicted it, and although it was of course what I was aiming for I never really believed that it would happen to me, again.

Eden debuted at Amazon.com with a lowly rank of around #60,000. I'd launched the book at $0.99 and £0.99 in the hope of enticing new readers to buy a Dean Crawford book for the first time, and upon seeing the rank I remember smiling to myself ruefully – there was no way I'd be retiring on that ranking.

But the next day Eden was at #40,000. The day after that, #20,000. Within a week the book had broken into the top #1,000 and a month later it peaked at a ranking of around #300, far higher than any of my traditionally published books had reached. By this time it was at full price and gaining reviews rapidly. I was earning about £200 per day from one book and could hardly believe that I'd struck gold at the first attempt with an Indie title.

What followed was a mad scramble to learn about digital advertising in order to promote the book further. I ran Countdown Deal promotions with Kindle Select, wrote blog posts, sought out blogger reviews and generally worked hard to promote Eden to new readers. The result was a book that remained a hit for several months, riding high in Amazon's charts around the world. Suitably enthused and already earning a very acceptable income as an author, I was well into writing the second book when I received a "cease and desist" letter from a legal firm in the USA. I was shocked to learn than a rival author had taken out a Trademark on the title "Eden" as a "work–of–fiction title" so that no other author could use that title in a series without opening themselves up to potential legal action.

I was stunned. I learned that I was one of several authors to receive the legal challenge, and that it was provoked by our various titles selling more than the author who had obtained the trademark. He had targeted us in the hopes that we would take our books down, in the mistaken belief that his own "Eden" would then rise to the top.

It was a crucial moment for me: I had never before encountered jealousy or spite from somebody who was supposed to be a fellow author. It taught me a valuable lesson: that for every one person who finds success, there will be a hundred who will do anything, no matter how ridiculous or cruel, to try to bring them down. I had a mortgage to pay, a family to feed and was new to the Indie scene. I didn't want to compromise what I'd achieved and risk future income fighting an author who was clearly aiming to bring down other authors by whatever means they could summon.

Despite all that Eden had achieved, I decided to abandon the series and move on. By this time I had another series idea, inspired by the fact that while traditional publishing had virtually abandoned science–fiction on the bookshelves, the genre was absolutely thriving in independent publishing. Many authors were forging great careers with space–opera novels and I wanted both to write in the genre and get in on the action. If that meant not approaching traditional publishers with my work, then so be it.

Just three years after earning my first real publishing deal, I was going fully independent...

XIV: Working for the man: life inside a publishing house.

Walking into the offices of a major publisher for the first time is an exciting experience, to say the least. You've finally crossed the invisible line between aspiring writer and professional author, and there are people working for your publisher who will do all that they can to help your career become the success story you've dreamed it will be.

However, there's a lot of work ahead. If you're under the impression that your life will now be a cosy one of delivering one manuscript per year while sipping champagne on a Caribbean island, you're in the wrong job.

My meetings with the editorial, marketing and Public Relations teams at *Simon & Schuster UK* in London were always fun and informative. My editor Maxine Hitchcock led the team that went on to shape my debut *Covenant* and the later books in the series. Despite all the editorial work that I had done on the book with my literary agent, more edits were required. For the next few months while writing the next book in the series, *Immortal*, I went through countless edits on *Covenant*. Every single line was scrutinized, which is hardly surprising considering the amount of money the publisher had just spent on me. Alternative titles were discussed, sample cover art images were considered, marketing meetings pored over the publisher's plans for the book with my agent by my side.

Throughout all of this, an author must remain professional and courteous to their publishing team. I did everything that was asked of me and only fought against changes that I did not agree with from a professional, not a personal, perspective. After a while, members of the team would confide that it was much easier to work with me than some of their other authors. I remember one member of the PR team introducing me to a new employee at the publisher, who would be working with me on one of my later books. As they approached, I overheard her talking softly to the newbie. Her exact words were;

'It's okay, Dean's one of the nice ones.'

I was both heartened and surprised by this. In all walks of life one meets awkward personalities, but awkward authors are considered by many publishing professionals as part and parcel of the business. *Divas*, as they were sometimes referred to, appear everywhere and often become somewhat agitated if they are not treated with the kind of "respect" that they believe they deserve.

Don't be one of those people. Work hard for your publisher, be kind to those in the offices when you visit and make yourself somebody whom they can work with. The reason for this is greater than just simple common sense and decency; just like literary agents, publishers *can* and *will* drop authors who prove too difficult to work with. I have heard many stories of authors who wouldn't perform edits or argued against all and any changes to their manuscript, and a few tales of authors who were rude and even aggressive toward publishing staff and literary agents. Such tantrums won't get you any friends in the business and despite the sheer volume of submissions received by agents and publishers, a nasty or rude author can stick in the memory for a very long time. You should always remember that publishers and agents talk to each other a lot…

Assuming that you all get along well, there will still be many differences of opinion over cover art, titles, whether or not you use your own name or whether a pen name (*nom de plume*) should be adopted and so on. For the most part the publishers know best and you should follow their lead. However, when it comes to titles and pen names they often think only in the short–term, with PR and marketing teams heavily influenced by what's "trendy" right now and the profits required for any given book to earn out its advance and make long–term profits for the company.

The harsh truth is that despite the fact that most people working in publishing companies do so because they love books, publishers are *businesses* and they exist to make money for owners and shareholders. At the time of writing it is a fact that the vast majority of published books do not earn out the advances their authors are paid, which means that those authors will never earn any further royalties from their books.

But how can that be? I hear you ask. *Surely they must eventually start earning a regular income from their books?* Well, no, actually, they don't. In this fast–moving world of ours it is often now said that a new book by a debut author has approximately a two–week shelf life, during which it must sink or swim. If it stays afloat and its sales seem promising, it will remain in place. If sales fall or don't meet expectations, the book is replaced on the shelves by the masterpiece of the next new author and sales plummet.

Many of todays' most powerful bestselling authors grew their brand in earlier decades when publishers still had the time to help build a career. A failed novel was not necessarily the end of the road and they would nurture a writer's career until their backlist was large enough and strong enough that they "broke out" and became an *overnight* hit. Thus, over years and even decades big names such as Lee Child, Peter James, James Rollins and others built their careers into multi–million dollar brands.

What is very interesting (or depressing, depending on how you look at it) is that with limited shelf space due to the now–reduced number of bookshops in most western countries, those bookshops will for commercial reasons only buy books by authors whom they know will sell. Therefore, they buy only the *big* names. Thus, the current crop of major best–sellers remain best–selling by virtue of the fact that there isn't enough room on the shelves for new voices to break through, and book sellers won't take financial chances on new books by new authors they don't know.

Catch 22: you can't get shelf space if you're not already a big name, and you can't become a big name without shelf space.

Add to this the fact that books can be "*remaindered*" – sent back to the publisher to be pulped if they don't sell, and that the introduction of supermarkets and other major chains into the bookselling realm has forced retail prices even further down, and you have a situation where the profit margin for traditionally published books is so small that publishers can rarely afford to take chances on new authors with no proven history of sales.

It is no surprise, considering the above, that most publishers make losses on books acquired by their editors. Advances are paid, the books are published a year or more later, they fail to sell in the numbers hoped for, the author does not receive a further contract and has to start all over again, and their treasured tome goes out of print. Worse, the publisher still holds the rights for that book for the contract period, sometimes as much as thirty–five years.

Some smart authors have *rights–reversion* clauses in their contracts, often negotiated by their agents, that if and when their books go out of print they get ownership of the full rights returned to them. Until the advent of digital and independent publishing this was a fairly common occurrence, but now the waters are muddied by vendors such as Amazon and its digital and print–on–demand services: can a paperback *ever* now be considered out of print?

Perhaps the most fortunate authors are those who sold titles for modest advances but then had an unexpected hit on their hands. Royalties flowed in for many years, giving them the opportunity to build a sizeable backlist before their star waned (if it did). Some, like me, earned tremendous advances but then ensured that we handled the money carefully, just in case the bubble burst.

Looking after your business.

One of the most helpful things my agent ever advised me to do in the wake of my first contract was to form a company and ensure that I had a second account set up, into which all taxes should be paid. The reason for this was that he had seen many authors squander their advances and then end up with a tax bill they couldn't pay when sales didn't meet the publisher's forecasts and they were dropped like a hot rock.

If you get a good deal, it is worth founding a company and setting up accounts so that you can tuck the advances away, but also suitable sums to cover those tax bills when they inevitably arrive. I would advise, if you're one of the lucky ones and your advances are suitably hefty, to hire an accountant to handle the money. My accountant ensures that I get the best deal possible while keeping my nose clean with the tax man, and the money he saves me doing this more than covers the cost of his work.

You don't know what's coming around the next corner, and if you've been following my story throughout this book you'll by now be aware that no matter how high you climb, you can still always fall again. Be prepared as much as you can be for failure to follow success, just like the characters in your novel, because you never know quite when that rug might be pulled from beneath your feet…

Final thoughts.

These and many other considerations make the future of traditional publishing uncertain across all genres, although it is expected that many avenues will remain for physical books: schools, non–fiction and children's books all have many good reasons to be available not just as e–books. But for fiction the paperback future is not so rosy. Yes, many people still love the feel of a *real* book, and it is also true that the youth of today are starting to suffer somewhat from a new and very modern affliction: *screen fatigue*. However, it is also equally true that children today are using physical books less as a reading medium and are becoming more used to using screens: screens are becoming the *norm* for the younger generation. The recent arrival of Virtual Reality in our living rooms and wearable–tech such as Microsoft's *Holo Lens* further provide new means of enjoying commercial fiction for busy people on the move. Holding on to your rights as an author, and having the flexibility to adopt new strategies and reach new readers rather than being left behind living from one hoped–for contract to another, is why an increasing number of authors are turning to independent publishing as a means to forging a career in this tough industry. This trend is not confined to those who have been unable to attract the attention of literary agents or publishers. I myself have voluntarily built an independent label for titles that didn't quite fit the mould for major publishing houses, and it has proven a very enjoyable and profitable career move.

The choice is yours. A major publishing house and a truly successful novel can turn even a debut author into a household name almost overnight and provide a level of fame and fortune that are hugely attractive. However, for every single author who has achieved this lofty goal there are countless thousands who never even got close.

The odds are against most authors who choose the traditional route, for no other reason than sheer numbers, the increasingly dated traditional publishing business model and the whims of fate. But if you're willing to work hard for yourself (and every traditional publisher will require you to do the same if you're signed to them anyway) and learn new skills beyond those required to simply write a novel, then independent publishing may be the path for you.

February 2014

For the last six months, my company had made a loss. The cost of living and the fact that my wife had been made redundant several months earlier meant that while we were not yet struggling due to the careful way in which we had handled the advances from my Simon & Schuster books, I was definitely concerned about the future.

After the success of Eden, sales had gradually dwindled until I was earning about £500 per month from my meagre list of three independent titles. I knew by now that I needed a proper series in place and with a fresh idea in mind and a firm plan laid out for the year, I embarked on my first space–opera series of science fiction novels.

I launched the Atlantia Series in March 2014 with Survivor. The novel was slower this time to gain ground than Eden, but gradually it picked up pace and by the time the sequel Retaliator was launched in June of that year I was starting to get moving. My earnings rapidly increased and by July 2014 I'd almost reached the point where I was earning the equivalent of my family's cost of living.

At that point, Amazon dropped a new bombshell with the introduction of Kindle Unlimited. KU, as it's now known, introduced the concept of "pages read", allowing Prime members of Amazon's flagship subscription service to download one Kindle Select book for free per month. Amazon would then pay the author per page of that book read. In one fell swoop, my sales and earnings were halved along with most other independent authors.

There was little that I or any other author could do about it, and despite endless hand–wringing and arguments on writing forums across the globe I decided that the best thing I could do was to just dig deep and keep going. Independent publishing to me was still the best bet for a long–term future as a full–time author, so abandoning the concept after so much hard work seemed pointless. I'd essentially reached the point of no return in my story: it would likely take me as long to go back and write another book to try to get a traditional publishing deal as it would to forge ahead and keep growing my readership via new indie titles.

However, in the interests of furthering my cause I wrote to Simon & Schuster and asked them for permission to continue on with my Ethan Warner series as an independent author. I reasoned that any success I had as an indie with future titles would also draw attention to the original books in the series, and thus would benefit us both. I'd been stung once by unjust legal challenges after the Eden debacle so I didn't want to risk another; "better safe than sorry" was my motto. Although it took six months for a reply to surface, the publisher finally let me know that it was fine by them.

With written confirmation that I could independently publish further Ethan Warner books under my own label, I set out to expand my independent brand beyond science fiction and into action and adventure, and that's where things really got going for me as an independent author.

XV Flying solo: Independent publishing in the digital age

There was once a time when self–publishing was a subject of scorn for those happily settled with literary agents and publishing deals. In some circles, it still is. In an industry were being business–like is the key to survival, the snobbery that still exists regarding independent publishing puzzles me somewhat. I have heard authors remark with disdain that they would never, ever, *ever* even *dream* of publishing a book with Amazon. What puzzles me the most is that the same authors bemoan their dwindling sales and advances from their publishers and lament the loss of space on bookshelves in shops across the country.

There is still an air of "*prestige*" about having been published by a major house, especially if that publication involved international deals, translations, movie rights and other wondrous bells and whistles. Some perhaps crave the lavish lifestyle led by the big names in traditional publishing, the sense of acceptance and of having arrived at a new level of success. For some that dream is realised, but for every author that "breaks out" and becomes a household name there are literally thousands who sink without trace or carve careers that never see them earn the living that they probably deserve.

The truth is that most authors, even best–sellers, do not make a full time living out of their writing. The oft–quoted income for the average author is around £10,000, hardly a living wage in this day and age. Yet the independent author has grown to become something of a spectre for major publishing houses. Increasingly, independent authors are out–earning their traditionally published brethren and in some cases are becoming as famous as even the biggest names. E. L. James, Hugh Howie, A. G. Riddle, J.A Konrath, Rachel Abbot and others have literally earned millions from their independent careers, often dallying with traditional contracts for a while before retreating by choice back to their independent labels.

So what's the difference, I hear some readers ask? So what if some people make millions but most make little – isn't that the same no matter what side of the publishing divide one decides to choose? Well, yes and no. The biggest difference between independent publishing and traditional publishing, in terms of income, is *how far up the ladder* you have to be in order to earn a *living wage*.

In traditional publishing, there is such a thing known as the "sales pyramid". The pyramid is effectively a sort of graph, with number of authors along the horizontal axis at the bottom and individual earnings along the vertical axis. At the top of the pyramid are the big earners, the household names who bring in millions of dollars of revenue. James Patterson probably sits at the very top of the pyramid with annual earnings in excess of twenty million dollars, thus representing the pinnacle of the sales pyramid: one person with massive earnings occupying a tiny pedestal at the very top. At the bottom of the pyramid are countless authors all earning next–to–nothing from their books. So far, so simple.

Somewhere in the middle of that pyramid are the authors who represent the "mid–list". This refers to authors making a living from their books, probably hitting the best–seller lists from time to time, but not having yet broken out with a truly major hit. This is where the real difference between traditional and independent publishing emerges. To hit the mid–list in the UK (as an example) as a traditionally published author requires sales of perhaps one thousand copies per day: the kind of figure that earns publishers enough in their share of the royalties to hang on to the author in question and keep renewing their contracts. These sales figures can see an author edge into the bestseller lists in the major newspapers.

Contrast this with the independent author selling just fifty of their books per day digitally. Because of the much higher royalty (up to seventy per cent), they find themselves netting around £100 per day, which is just over £36,000 per year. If *they* were selling a thousand copies per day, they would be earning an incredible £700,000 per year (and yes, independent authors garnering those kinds of sales do exist). The message here is simple: an independent author can potentially make a living on *far lower sales* than a traditionally published author, and it's this midlist author that interests me more than the big hitters.

I'm going to treat you to a lushly illustrated image to better portray the pecking order of the two methods of publishing. Below the "mid–list" lines in the pyramids, an author cannot make a living, whereas in or above it they can.

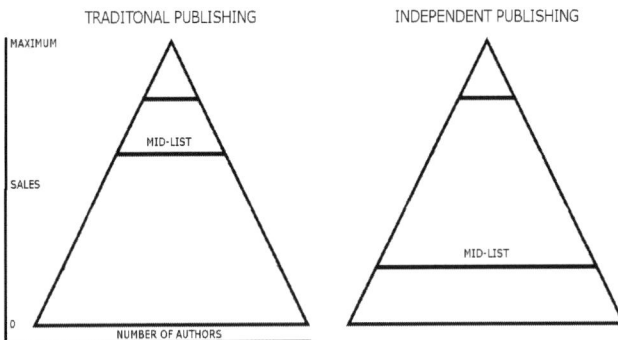

When you've recovered from the lavish nature of this diagram, you'll notice that it is a simplified snap–shot of publishing incomes but none the less paints a clear picture of the reality that independent publishing has brought to the industry.

What is most interesting is the sheer numbers of independent authors making a living when contrasted with those signed solely to traditional contracts. We often see in the newspapers sensationalised articles on the big earners and the incomes they make, but there are literally thousands of independent authors you've never heard of now making a great living as writers who have never (or were unable) to get anywhere near a literary agent let alone a publishing house. Selling fifty books per day would likely see a traditionally published author's books pulled and their contracts dropped in the blink of an eye because the numbers simply cannot support the traditional publishing model – there just isn't enough profit. But an independent author selling fifty books a day for the first time would likely be singing happy songs and doing cartwheels around their garden while sipping *Pimms*, knowing that they're earning the equivalent of a great salary while doing a job that they love in the comfort of their own homes.

I have given talks at the *International Thriller Writers* convention in London, chatted to other authors endlessly at conventions in the UK, and although I hear them agreeing with me and nodding enthusiastically I know of few at the time of writing who have managed to overcome the uncertainty (and understandable fear) of breaking away from their publishing houses and literary agents and going it alone. Of the few that have, all have seen the light within a book or two as their sales start to increase and they see money coming in as if from nowhere.

The potential, as well as the pitfalls, are widely documented but I think that it's important to add that for the majority of authors self–publishing can be as much of a disappointment as traditional publishing. The weighty burdens of self–marketing, low rankings and meagre earnings can quickly give rise to despondency as the hopeful author realises that it's no easier in self–publishing than it is in the traditional publishing world. At the time of writing there are an estimated 1,800,000 books published on Amazon, so getting noticed is just as difficult as it is in traditional publishing. Of course many of those millions of titles are poorly written, barely edited and with dull covers designed by *wannabees* hoping to take advantage of the self–publishing dream. You're not one of them, you're a professional. But just like traditional publishing there is a need to stand out from the endless crowd: in short, your work needs to be of the same standard that you would be happy to submit to a publisher as part of a contract.

In addition, like traditional publishing the independent world has trends – things go in and out of favour. Children's books and Young Adult titles struggle a bit and horror is also a tough genre in which to break out. In contrast crime, action and adventure, post–apocalyptic, science fiction and romance are flying. However, those trends do not necessarily preclude the success or failure of a particular title: no longer confined to bookshelves, there will always be a willing market for your book out there somewhere. It doesn't matter if it's your life–long passion to pen an epic series about the leader of a nomadic tribe of nyphomaniac–zombie–ninja– Amazonian–shape–shifters called Daphne: there is likely an audience for it somewhere. With millions of Kindles, PCs, Macs and various *i*Gadgets out there able to display your e–book, as long as interested people can find it they will buy it, provided it is professionally presented.

Another thing that truly separates independent publishing from traditional is the fact that no matter what genre is in vogue right now, your book *will be published*. It will never be pulped or pulled from the shelves and at any time you can edit it, alter the cover and otherwise improve the title in order to adapt to new trends as they appear. *Full control* is the big advantage of Indie publishing, something that scant few authors experience with traditional houses, but it's the earning capacity from just a few sales that traditional publishers don't want authors to truly understand. If they did, traditional publishing's business model would implode catastrophically overnight.

So, if you're in the position that independent publishing is the route you have chosen, or you've exhausted all other options and there's nowhere else for your book to go and it's gathering digital dust on your hard drive, read on.

XVI: Oh crap, here we go then… Getting started as an Indie.

One of the things that initially convinced me to give Indie publishing a whirl were the comments of many of the editors who rejected my novel *Eden*: virtually all of them mentioned how much they enjoyed reading it. It does make me suspect sometimes that it was not the editors doing the rejecting but the marketing departments. However, the compliments gave me some confidence that I had not created a 100,000 word failure: maybe it really was the publishers who were making the mistake?

Call me a control–freak, but I've always been very independent and the idea of shelling out money on book production seemed crazy when with a bit of time and *effort* I could do it myself. The days of paying thousands of pounds for a hundred shabby looking vanity books are well and truly over, and if money is short then doing–it–all–yourself is a great alternative.

However should you wish or *need* to hire editors, cover–designers and so on then there are many reputable services available. Indeed if you're not experienced in self–editing, cover design and such like then I recommend doing so, because one thing that propels novels to success in independent publishing is a *professional* look. You wouldn't buy a car that looks like ten–thousand loose parts flying in close formation, so don't expect people to buy your book unless it is top–notch in every respect.

For some authors this process may simple be too daunting to approach. Going from your first novel to complete control of your publishing destiny is understandably a tough call to make. To answer this need, many independent publishing companies have risen who offer authors the chance to offload these tasks in return for a royalty payment.

Similar to traditional publishing contracts, these companies none the less provide a different approach with differing royalty contracts that are usually far better than those typically provided by traditional houses. They do not, however, pay an advance. If marketing, cover design and editorials really are just too much to bear, you could approach a company such as *Bookouture* in the hopes of achieving the success you've dreamed of. Be aware though that, just like traditional publishers, you're signing rights away for an extended period of time so you need to be certain that you're in the right hands.

However, if you're willing to give it a shot on your own here's what you'll need and it's all *free*!

You'll need to read this excellent guide on converting your book to HTML format:

http://guidohenkel.com/2010/12/take-pride-in-your-ebook-formatting/

You'll need the free Notepad++ to convert the book to HTML format, found here:

https://notepad-plus-plus.org/

I then use the free *Calibre* software to convert the HTML into Kindle's .mobi format;

https://calibre-ebook.com/

And this is simply the best freeware art package I've ever used (and I'm an ex–graphic designer). I use this for all my cover artwork.

https://www.gimp.org/

That's it as far as converting your novel for independent publishing goes, honest! You may also find it useful to join writer's forums on both the Internet and Facebook. There are many groups available and the best bet is to search around and find one that suits you.

The Nitty Gritty.

So, your manuscript is ready for conversion. Friends and family have read it, you've edited it until you're seeing the pages in your dreams and there's just nothing you can think of that will improve the work further. It's time to get it ready to send out into the world, so here are a few comments about the process of preparing your novel (we'll deal with the issue of *where* to publish your new indie title shortly).

Conversion.

Some independent authors will allow Amazon's in built converter to convert their book to the required format, or use Calibre's Word–to– .mobi converter. *Don't.* Both will be a bog–standard conversion with no author bibliography or dedication, no nuthin'. You want it to be better than that, right? Take the time to learn about how HTML works using Guido's step–by–step guide and using Calibre's advanced functions to control the Table of Contents. Create a page before the novel starts listing your copyright details, publication date, a link to your website and the logo of your company if you have one. Name your agent if you have one in case a publisher or editor reads the book and wants to make contact with them.

Learning to convert a novel to HTML takes a bit of time and practice but once you're on your way you'll learn to love it as I have. More to the point, if you pay for some other company to do this for you what happens if a reader spots a major flaw in your otherwise perfect tome? If you've done the work yourself, it can be edited and reposted to Amazon in minutes. If not, you're paying for someone else to do it all over again.

Make the *effort* to learn this process, and you'll never look back.

Cover Design

This can be tricky for many people. Although as authors we're all creatively minded, strong visual design is not a skill that can generally be acquired quickly. I was lucky in having been a graphic designer for ten years prior to writing full–time, so the process came easily to me. Here is an appallingly shameless plug of some of my *Indie* covers, all created by me using GIMP. Note the purposeful series similarity in some of the designs.

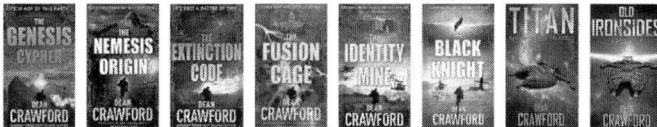

The idea is that your covers should look like they were designed by a major publishing house. In fact, *everything* about your book should say that. There are designers out there who will do the work for you but it can be expensive, so be willing to again put some effort into your presentation because *covers sell books*. If a reader sees a dull cover, trust me, they won't bother looking further to see if it's their kind of book. Would you? It's a bit like approaching a literary agent or an editor – one mistake and they'll move on because they haven't got time to mess about. If the author can't get a simple submission right, what's the chance that the rest of the manuscript will be amazingly good? Customers will act in a similar way.

Spending either time or money here, like editing, will pay dividends later.

Amazon exclusive or "go wide"?

As an independent author you have two choices; publish your book widely on Kobo, Kindle, Smashwords, iBookstore, CreateSpace (for paperbacks) and ACX (

audiobooks) *and* on your own website, all of which require slightly different approaches; or throw your lot in with Amazon via their Kindle Direct Publishing *Select* program.

Nowhere on Internet forums about independent publishing will you see more polarised views on any subject than this. Ignore all the crap spouted by those saying that "their way is the only way to go". To go wide or go exclusive with Amazon are both equally valid paths, it simply depends on yourself as an author, what kind of book you've written and your long–term goals as an author.

There are all kinds of pros and cons, but I chose *Select* and at the time of writing I'm an Amazon exclusive author. If you choose the same path then as well as earning from your standard book sales you'll be a part of Amazon's Kindle Lending Library, which allows people to borrow your book rather than buying it and earns you money for each page read. There are also other benefits to tempt authors into the scheme such as the ability to run "*Countdown*" deals, whereby you get to reduce the price of your books for a few days while still retaining the seventy per cent royalty rate, and *Select* titles gain preference from Amazon in rankings, where sales and pages read both contribute, and if you're lucky Amazon sometimes offers successful books the chance of a promotion backed and sponsored by them. The downside to being a part of Amazon KDP Select is that you cannot publish your book *anywhere* else, including your own website. You're a part of the Amazon family, but each term for each book in the program is ninety days so if *Select* doesn't seem to work for you it doesn't take long to pull titles out and go wide with them later.

The short answer in my experience is that as most platforms now have *apps* that allow Kindle titles to be read on them, there's really not much to be gained by going through the long slog of releasing your title on multiple platforms except for the old adage that you don't want to keep "all of your eggs in one basket". Authors who are wide usually stay there once success is found, but what keeps me in *Select* at this time is the fact that no other vendor can equal Amazon when it comes to readers finding books. In truth I'm already on all the other sites with my *Simon & Schuster* titles, so if I did decide to go wide I'd already have a platform.

An oft–recommended path for a new author is to launch a book with Amazon KDP Select to take advantage of their promotional offers, Kindle Library features and the easy of having everything in once place, and then start going wide once the author has two or three books in place. It's when you have a strong backlist of titles that going wide seems to make more sense, but be aware that it's harder to gain traction on other sites than it is with Amazon so be prepared to advertise the hell out of your books once you step into the realm of other vendors and your own website sales.

Digital distributors.

One easy way to go wide in a hurry is to use digital distributors such as *Smashwords* or *Draft2Digital*. For a cut of your royalties, these distributors offer a simple service that allows you to publish your books on *i*Bookstore, Amazon, Kobo etc in one go, simplifying the process further. The obvious downside to this process is that you lose a little income each time that you do it, and it's tough to backtrack later and re–publish directly with each vendor as the book has to be taken down, losing it valuable ranking and possibly any reviews gained too.

Amazon Affiliate Scheme

This is a tool used by Amazon to expand its reach when shoppers buy books via the links you advertise on your website. If your books have a link and they click on it, Amazon pays you a small fee, and also pays you another fee based on anything else that customer buys from Amazon over the next twenty–four hours.

This remarkably efficient little scheme means that if you're getting a lot of traffic on your website and one of those people buy one of your books via your links to Amazon, and then they go buy a 60" plasma television in the next twenty–four hours, you'll get a cut of everything. You're leaving money on the table if you're not a part of this, and it requires you only to place an Amazon tracking pixel behind each link on your site. Simples.

Marketing.

The bottom line is that how much marketing you do will depend somewhat on your backlist. I firmly believe that my success was down to three things; firstly and most importantly, novels that are professionally presented in all respects; secondly, a strong backlist of traditionally published titles; and thirdly, a low promotional launch price. (It's worth noting that *Eden* climbed up into the Top 1,000 in Paid Kindle USA without *any* advertising, which I hadn't bothered with because I didn't believe I'd even chart out there as I was less well known.) It was only when I saw the book's meteoric rise that I belatedly started buying digital advertising to capitalise on the success. Therefore the book's unexpected rise can only really have been down to the presentation and genre.

1) *Presentation and backlist.*

Assuming your cover is sorted, you need to think now about your blurb, the brief synopsis of the story. The best thing to do here is to look at other best–sellers in your chosen genre and effectively emulate their style. Again, time spent getting this right is well rewarded. If, like me, you spend about a week poring over every single detail, you'll be doing it right. Here's the blurb from my science fiction novel "*Survivor*";

A civilisation destroyed. A species doomed to wander the cosmos. A lone survivor feared by all, her voice silenced and her face veiled behind a metal mask.

The Atlantia is all that remains of humanity: a former military fleet frigate turned prison–ship now hunted by a terrifying force and haunted by escaped convicts threatening the survival of her beleaguered crew and civilians.

Trapped in orbit around a foreign world, damaged and low on supplies, the crew of the Atlantia are forced to make a deal with the devil to forge an alliance of murderous convicts, exhausted soldiers and terrified civilians in a last–ditch attempt to confront the technological horror that has consumed mankind.

Humanity's last stand begins here, and only one woman stands between annihilation and our future…

Survivor is the first volume of the science fiction "Atlantia" space opera series from internationally best–selling thriller and action adventure author Dean Crawford.

You'll notice also that when you upload a book to Amazon's KDP, you have a section for reviews. This is where I get a bit "creative" with my independent books. Careful to remain honest, I list reviews with the header: *"Praise for Dean Crawford."* Cunning as a fox, this allowed me to list reviews I've received over the years from the *Wall Street Journal, Melbourne Age, Sun, Kirkus, Publisher's Weekly* etc. Readers can recognise such publications and may be convinced to give your book a try. So if you've had reviews from those or similar publications, use them!

2) *Backlist*

This is down to you. When you join KDP and Author Central, if you haven't already, you'll have the chance to add your new title and create the page. Not all readers will visit this page, but it provides a great over–view of your work and your history as an author. If you have already published several books with high review ratings, it'll give a potential new reader confidence that they're buying something worthwhile.

Here's a link to mine:

https://www.amazon.co.uk/Dean–Crawford/e/B004UO651U/ref=ntt_athr_dp_pel_1

Notice my use of links to my Twitter account, forthcoming books on my Author Description, and videos made to promote my novels.

3) *Price.*

I cannot emphasise enough how important it is to recognise that the self–publishing market works in reverse compared to the traditional model, especially if you're writing in a genre for which you're not known. To initially attract readers you need to price your books *low*. Some independent authors even make their first title *free* to draw readers in. I think that this is sometimes a step too far when it comes to placing the book on Amazon or other vendors for free. Sure, it may get readers to download your book, but if somebody wandered up to you and offered you for free something that had taken months or even years to create you'd probably wonder what they'd been smoking.

I provide a free book on my website and via digital advertising in return for potential new readers to sign up to my mailing list (more on all of this soon). The book remains for sale on Amazon (although not via Select, of course) so it still earns me money, but it also can draw in long–term fans of my books. Essentially, the book is earning double for me. I view simply handing out free books for absolutely nothing in return as something that only totally unknown, fully–independent authors should do in order to launch their careers, and for those who have done so in the past it has proven an effective method.

I prefer a different approach to the process of enticing new readers to my books. I launch a novel at a very attractive promotional price for maybe a week or two to bring new readers in, say £0.99 in the UK and $0.99 in the USA. If the presentation, cover and blurb all look good this will help to bring new readers to your book and send it climbing the charts quickly. Another cheeky tactic is to buy your own book while simultaneously buying the current best–seller in your Amazon category: this ensures that you'll show up on the list of *"customers also bought"* for that best–selling title, getting your name alongside theirs for a brief period.

Some are saying that books priced this low are now going out of fashion, and that quality is more important. Amazon's *Select* program also has services such as "Countdown Deals" that allow for discounting. They're worth considering, but to start with give your book the best chance and launch it with an attractive price. Make sure that you state this at the head of your book description, letting your potential new reader know that they should really buy your book *now* and not later on, when they'll miss out on the bargain.

Paperbacks and Audiobooks

As an independent author, you'll be required to look after your paperback and audiobooks too. For paperbacks, Amazon's *Createspace* is a fine vendor of print-on–demand titles. You simply convert your novel into the page format that *Createspace* requires, adjust your cover art accordingly and select where you want the novel to be sold and at what price. Amazon does the rest and it's a very easy process.

For Audiobooks things are a little more complex. ACX, which is also run by Amazon, is your place to go. Here, you have two options:

1) Hire a narrator and split the royalties from the audiobook.

2) Pay up–front for the whole recording.

Splitting the royalties is the route that most authors take, for the simple reason that most decent narrators charge around $200 – $300 per finished hour, and some twice as much as that. A typical audiobook of one of my standard 100,000 word titles thus costs about $2,400 to complete. Major financial investment like this at the beginning of a career is not always the wisest move when an author is still trying to build their audience.

Although I choose to pay up front, because of the long–term earnings from those books in the future, it's a major expense even for me. The reason I do so is because audiobooks are the fastest growing sector of fiction at the time of writing, and the potential earnings for an audiobook over the life of the author can be considerable. With an ACX author taking a forty per cent royalty and audiobooks selling for at least $10, it doesn't take all that many sales to earn out the cost of production.

If you can definitely afford up–front production costs, then go for it. If not, royalty share is a perfectly acceptable route and will ensure that you get those audiobooks up there alongside your e–book and paperback. Don't forget to link them all on your website too, to catch that all important Amazon Affiliate income!

February 2015

The first title in my newly branded Warner & Lopez series, "The Nemesis Origin", was launched in February 2015 and this time I found myself with an instant success story on my hands. Following on from the original Simon & Schuster titles but with a new story arc, the books gained ground in the charts almost as quickly as my enthusiasm for independent publishing. A sequel, "The Fusion Cage" followed in May 2015, "The Identity Mine" in August and "The Black Knight" in October. With four books in the series and the five Atlantia Series books also doing well I was finally on my way. My monthly earnings increased month on month from April 2015 onward, and by Christmas 2015 I was earning an average of around £5,000 per month in sales and pages read. But I still felt as though I could do something better than other authors in the space opera genre, and an idea for a new series that had popped into my mind that year became my new launch in early 2016.

"Old Ironsides", the first in a new space opera series that mixed science fiction with crime fighting, launched in January 2016 and became my first truly massive Indie hit. Following the adventures of Nathan Ironsides, a former Denver cop who awakens in the 24th Century after being placed in cryogenic storage in 2016, the book was the first time that I broke into Amazon.com's Top #100 with a full–price title. In a single month I earned more than my entire first year of independent publishing and finally cemented my place as a truly successful independent author. More than that, I had proven what a lot of industry experts said could not be done: I had built a viable, full–time career selling books that cost less than a cup of coffee.

The rest of 2016 saw further titles launched in both the Old Ironsides series and the Warner & Lopez series, before I started to think about focusing more of my time on advertising. By September 2016 I had no less than eighteen titles on my independent Fictum label, a terrific output to have produced over just three years, yet many of those titles were only selling a handful of copies per day. The output, or backlist as it's known, was there but not enough people were seeing the books. I knew without a shadow of a doubt that there were countless more readers out there who would love my books if only they could all see them. To that end, I decided that 2017 would be the year where I would finally slow down on the writing of my books and start to invest money back into my business to produce advertising that would take my books out of their digital shelves and place them in front of the kind of readers who wanted to read them.

But first, I would write a book about everything I'd learned on my long journey, because so many people had asked me the same question and I could never remember to tell them everything at once because there's so much to learn.

"How do I go about doing what you've done?"

XVII: Look at me! Selling yourself

When I released *Eden*, being an amateur at the independent publishing game, I did absolutely no marketing whatsoever. It was only as the book raced up the charts that I got behind the title and started cultivating a "buzz" around it.

There were two ways I did this. In the UK I contacted enthusiastic bloggers who over the years had reviewed my *Ethan Warner* titles for *Simon & Schuster,* and asked them if they'd like to look at *Eden*. Bloggers are hugely busy but always lovely, and many agreed. Their reviews hit Amazon days or weeks later and drove the title further up the charts.

In the USA, not knowing any bloggers there, I opted for purchased advertising when I realised that such a thing was actually possible. There are a number of places that this can be done and depending on your budget you can buy banners, Facebook ads, website ads and so on that can, potentially, reach tens of thousands of new readers. Some of the top places can be found listed at the back of this book under the "Links" page. Various deals can be found, with banners on Indie writing forums like *KBoards* going for as little as $25, and single adverts on *BookBub* costing $600 plus for coverage in the UK and USA. My recommendation would be to buy cheaper ads first, and then if your book starts gaining traction you can invest in your own success and get something more expensive.

Your website

I'm going to assume that you're not reading this inside a mud hut in Namibia and that, as an author who is soon to be published one way or the other, you have a website. If not, get one. There are many ways in which you can cheaply do this, and with services such as *Wordpress* providing easy ways to build simple websites it should not take you long to get sorted.

Make sure that if you have already got a free book to offer prospective readers in return for them signing up to your mailing list (more on that below) and that the freebie is advertised boldly on your website. Here's a link to my website so you can see what I mean;

http://www.deancrawfordbooks.com/

Advertising on Amazon, Facebook and Twitter

As the growth of digital advertising has become more and more a factor in how books become visible to readers, so vendors of all kinds have jumped on the bandwagon with their own versions of paid advertising.

Facebook was arguably the first to do this, with Amazon and Twitter following behind when the success of the process was finally realised. Essentially, unlike subscription based services, companies like Facebook have sufficient data on their many billions of users that they can provide a service that can target adverts with almost laser–guided precision to sections of the public who have expressed a "liking" for the items featured in said adverts.

So, as an author you can use Facebook to target fans of a similar, successful author and entice those readers to check out your books. Each person that clicks on your advert results in a (hopefully) small charge called a Cost–Per–Click. By careful management of your adverts, it is possible to attract interested members of the public to your books and your mailing list and at the same time continuously refine and improve those adverts in many countries across the world.

Some authors have seen spectacular success with these methods of advertising, and it's also fair to add that the majority do not. However, with careful use it is possible to maintain a sensible expenditure while reaching new customers across the globe, and even to make a profit doing so.

The best place to learn about this process in depth is the *Self–Publishing Formula* course, run by British author Mark Dawson, who used Facebook advertising to build a tremendous mailing list and a bestselling career as a crime author. The course covers everything you need to know through a series of step–by–step videos, and also has Twitter and YouTube advertising sections for those dipping their toe into those platforms. The course costs several hundred dollars and only opens a couple of times per year, but if you're serious about building mailing lists and your brand awareness, there is no better place to start. A link can be found at the end of this book.

To be a part of any of these you'll need to have a Twitter account and a Facebook account. You'll need to do this yourself, but it need not be the nightmare that some authors have endured. Get your website and Amazon Author Page sorted along with the Twitter account, Facebook Fan Page and a blog if you wish, and then ensure that they all link together as much as possible. Like many I don't much enjoy all the social media and marketing side of things, but in this modern and digital age it's *essential* to at least have a presence. They're all free so don't waste them. Just like traditional publishing, independent publishing is all about getting yourself and your titles visible. You don't have to spend 24 hours a day on the Internet, just a bit of time in the evening will do to keep your presence alive – it's about all I can manage.

Whatever you do, don't get a *"robot"* service to run your Twitter account. I see a lot of authors "following" 50,000 other authors, who are all likewise "following" them back. Except that none of them are following *anybody*. They're all just tweeting about their own books to each other and nobody is listening. It's the Internet's equivalent of a mad person shouting in the street. I only follow about 500 people on Twitter and even then I barely see anything they write, there are just too many posts. Focus on those who matter: *your readers*. Try always to reply to them and be a *real* person. Believe me, it'll gain you far more followers than the carpet–bombing technique used by so many supposedly bestselling authors endlessly telling readers how wonderful their books are. If their books were *that* wonderful and selling *so* well, they wouldn't have to keep tweeting about it…

Follow like–minded readers and authors, talk to them, enjoy it and learn from it. Make sure your various web pages have images of your books and things to talk about, and let your audience grow steadily. It's worth it. Sometimes when I tweet about a newly released book that message is often re–tweeted by my followers to (potentially) in excess of 20,000 people at a time. That's a BIG potential audience and as I said, it's all *free*.

Mailing List.

Probably the most important thing that you'll need to build as an independent author is a mailing list. Having fans and followers whom you can notify *directly* about new book launches and special promotions and have a more personalised relationship with can be the difference between good sales and tremendous sales. At the time of writing I have about 2,000 subscribers on my list, which is growing steadily day by day. I know of some authors who have lists 50,000 strong and who can launch a new book directly into the Top #500 at Amazon on the first day using just their mailing list.

You can use various mailing list hosts, but I use MailChimp as it's the one I've grown used to. Free up to a certain number of subscribers, and only charging small fees for 1,000 and beyond, MailChimp can be synchronized with other platforms such as Facebook and Twitter to provide a uniform platform with which to build your list. The customisable nature of those lists and the ease by which they can be used to develop mailing campaigns make them an essential aid to building your reader platform and brand.

How do I build my list though?

Well, the best and simplest way to do that is to offer your potential readers something for free. That's where my uncertainty over placing books for free at Amazon comes in. Unless you have enough titles to give away books for free, the best way to build your personalised audience is to offer them a free book in return for signing up to your mailing list. Make them give you something in return for that free book.

Although many authors argue that this process merely attracts freeloaders, it's been proven that the lists generated are actually full of highly–engaged readers who have enjoyed your free book and will go on to buy others in your list. Yes, there are always some freeloaders about but they're generally in the minority and besides, they'll get their fix from all the absolutely free books at Amazon and others without having to sign up to your list. Offering a free book in return for signing up is the best incentive to finding and holding on to new readers and building that audience that one day will help you launch books into the publishing stratosphere.

While you can set up a free book download via your Mailchimp account using the "automation" feature, there are also vendors who for a small monthly fee can provide excellent platforms for authors looking for new readers of their free books. *Instafreebie* and *BookFunnel* are two of the best known examples, and links can be found at the end of this book. Both vendors provide a service that immediately downloads your freebie to new fans' e–readers in exchange for their signing up to your mailing list. There's no fuss and it's a one–page process that converts readers into fans. Get your freebie up onto those platforms, and if you're lucky or just work plain hard then your book might be selected for one of their free promotions, which can net you thousands of subscribers in just a matter of days.

Getting reviews.

Often considered one of the hardest parts of the business, and this is where your marketing and approaching bloggers comes in. I once did a back–of–the–envelope calculation and figured out that about 0.3% of readers left reviews on books that they'd read on Amazon. So, roughly speaking an author has to sell about 300 copies to get a single review. When you're just starting off that's no easy task.

There has been a huge amount of press in the recent past about *"sock–puppets"* – authors creating accounts to review their own books, or (worse) denigrate the work of rival authors. In my mind, an author asking mum and dad to review their book to get it off the ground is not such an evil thing. If mum and dad lie out of kindness and give their offspring's poor book a five–star rating, then sooner or later genuine readers will expose the deception. It's self–regulating to some degree. On the other hand, fake reviews by rival authors designed to cull sales of competitor's novels is downright underhanded (I once had one removed by Amazon, written by a rival Indie author in my genre who did a very poor job of covering their tracks).

This is where your mailing list and your Facebook pages can come in handy. If you develop a following before your first book is published, perhaps due to your presence on writing forums or blog posts about your writing journey (as I once did) then when you do come to launch your book there can be a surprising amount of moral support behind you that can convert into reviews as fellow authors read your book.

The best thing to do is to advertise your name and brand widely using your various free Internet feeds (Facebook, Twitter etc) and hope that followers of your efforts will help to get the ball rolling. I have several die–hard *Ethan Warner* fans, bless them, who read everything I do and often review the novels on Amazon. They like my work and offer their reviews honestly (not always 5–star, for instance). Add to this your approaches to suitable bloggers and, fingers crossed, you'll soon have a few reviews up to help your sales.

Note: It's worth approaching bloggers early – many are working parents with busy lives and long TBR lists from big publishing houses. You need their reviews up soon after your launch, so be ready to send your work to them at a moment's notice. It worked well for me.

Finally, that all important mailing list can be used to offer your biggest fans the chance to become both proof readers and ARC readers (Advance Reader Copies). A method used by traditional publishing, ARCs are sent out to super–fans and bloggers before the launch of the book. They read the book ahead of publication, and then when the book goes live they place their reviews, giving all–important social proof of the book's quality early in its shelf life.

Amazon and most vendors, at the time of writing, support the use of ARC readers. However, it appears that they're willing to take down reviews if they appear too quickly, in an attempt to stamp out the scamming of paid–review companies (see below). So, be measured in your choices and perhaps have no more than half a dozen ARC readers to avoid incurring the wrath of Amazon, who are known sometimes to use a sledgehammer to kill a fly.

Paid reviews.

Don't. *Just don't.* It's against the Terms of Service of pretty much every vendor out there and is in effect "cheating". No matter how tempting it may seem, or how legitimate the companies providing these reviews may seem, ignore them like the plague. Amazon frequently blitzes reviews from such companies, erasing them from author's books (and sadly sometimes from the books of entirely innocent authors) and they also pursue legal cases against the companies. Authors have seen their KDP accounts permanently closed as a result of such activities, and that's a market share you don't want to lose. Leave such sites to the short–lived scammers and stick to the rules.

In the case of respected publications like *Kirkus Reviews* and *Publisher's Weekly* it's a slightly different ball game. The reviews are not cheap and they are only generally read by industry figures rather than your average reader, so the gain of a good review in either is limited by what your goal happens to be. If you want to entice the interest of major publishing houses then feel free to pay for one of these reviews. If, on the other hand, like me you're more interested in your readers then you're better off working to get your books into the hands of fans via digital marketing and let them do the reviewing for you.

The launch!

So, launch day has arrived!

Here is a simple time–table that encapsulates what I do just prior to, during, and after the launch of a new book on my Indie label. This is fairly typical of me, although budgets do change and advertisers also change depending on which ones are working best at any given time.

1. One month before launch: start sharing cover–art for the new title on my Facebook and Twitter pages, with launch dates and info.

2. Two weeks before launch: Mailing list shot to all subscribers, letting them know about the upcoming launch. Find and book paid advertising on subscription sites, planning dates to spread the launch over about seven days. Ideally, the best advertisers are in the centre of the launch period, the weaker ones at either end. This is to sustain the highest possible sales over the period, without generating too high a spike at Amazon, thus getting the best out of their algorithms. Send the book to proof readers for a final check through.

3. One week before launch: Send the book to ARC readers with a review request, if they should wish to leave one.

4. Launch Day! I publish the book the day *before* the allotted date, in case there's any problem with Amazon, at the low launch price promised to my fans and followers. I then split my mailing list into four equal–sized chunks, based on their "star–rating" of how engaged they are with my mails. I target the lowest rated on day one, the three stars on day two, four stars on day three and then the most engaged five–star readers with the final mail on day four.

5. Stay active! Use Twitter, Facebook and all other social media platforms. Reply to e–mails about the launch, check that purchased digital adverts are running and watch my sales graph for the book to see which ads are working well.

6. Cross fingers! Take a break, and hope the book flies when the price goes up at the end of the promotional launch period.

I've got a one–star review from somebody who hated my book! What do I do?!

You move on and you say *nothing*. Some authors say that you haven't arrived until you've got your first one–star review. I've had plenty; some are just and concise critiques of my work, others are one–star reviews for entirely different products placed erroneously on my books, others still are blatant attacks designed to cull sales of the book in question, although these are much rarer nowadays. You can ask Amazon to remove genuinely unfair or erroneous reviews, but you'll most likely be ignored. Whatever you do, don't engage the reviewer. I've done this on occasion in the past when inaccurate reviews have unfairly maligned my books, but all you get is an endless stream of messages back and forth because, let's face it, everybody's both an expert and courageous when they can hide behind the Internet. If the review is poorly judged, let new readers decide and downvote the offending review.

If you happen to be on the receiving end of such a review soon after your book has launched, it can be a terrible blow but push on through and keep going. If in doubt, just visit the Amazon page of what you consider to be the very *best* book you've ever read and you'll doubtless find one star reviews of that book too. Everybody gets them, and so will you. Rise above them, take any sensible criticisms seriously and edit the book accordingly if you agree with the critique, and keep moving forward. Engaging reviewers on the Internet rarely ends well.

Can I make a career of independent publishing alongside traditional contracts?

Quite possibly. The independent publishing world is now mimicking the traditional publishing market in that a tiny number of authors occupy the top of the sales list with huge numbers of copies sold, while the vast majority lie in obscurity far down the rankings. You'll see on writer's forums that many Indie authors get wildly excited when they sell a copy of their book. Yes, a *single* copy. When somebody sells twenty copies in a day they virtually spontaneously combust, so frantically excited are their posts. However, there are countless authors who make their living entirely from independent works, occupying a small band just below the *mega–sellers* but far ahead of the rest of the pack. This is what you should aim for initially, a steady income from your books that you can take seriously. Whether you achieve this with your first book or you ninth is irrelevant – if you're a true professional about it, it's within your reach. Imagine what will happen if all three books in your debut trilogy are each selling just 50 copies a day at the 70% royalty rate a couple of years from now? Or all *nine* books in your epic series are selling fifteen copies per day? The only limits are your time, your effort and your audience, and in principal at least your audience with all forms of publishing is almost limitless.

But what about literary agents? Won't they hate me doing this?

I suspect that the best literary agents have by now realised and accepted not only that independent publishing has permanently changed the way that new writing talent can emerge, but are actively becoming involved in it. I know of several *Indie* authors who have been courted by literary agents and gone on to sign with them and obtain publishing deals. Often these are with Amazon's imprints such as *Thomas & Mercer* and *47North*, which creates a bit of a "false–positive", but not always. Matthew Mather recently sold the film rights to his *Indie* novel *CyberStorm* to a major Hollywood studio. Multi–million selling independent author Hugh Howie negotiated a deal for the paperback rights to his *Wool* and *Dust* serials while hanging on to the digital rights. E.L James's truly awful *Fifty Shades* series needs no mention really, but she did start out with the series as an Indie author until she was picked up by a traditional publisher.

Amazon is, in some respects, acting a bit like an agent in that the best of the next generation of Indie writers are rising to the top and being picked up for traditional contracts as they go. Authors already represented by agents who achieve strong sales of their books have provided their agent with great leverage when approaching traditional publishers with the title: a book that's already sold 20,000 copies is a far safer bet for sales and marketing teams than an unknown and untested new author with no revenue behind them. Un–agented independent authors can approach literary agents with sales figures to prove their worth and give the agent some idea of whether the book's got legs if the current publishing market fits the title.

Okay, smarty pants. If you're so good at this, why haven't you gone fully independent?

Because I'm not an idiot.

Publishers are always going to be there, and for all their flaws I like working with traditional houses. They have the power to turn an independent or even an unknown author into a global brand, and success in their world can often lead into television and movie rights.

Would I sign a traditional publishing deal again? Yes, in a New York Minute. However, the position I'm in now gives me much greater leverage over how the deal looks. Unlike back in 2010, I would have to consider how much money any one title I write could earn me as an Indie book over the course of, say, twenty–five years. Does the advance a publisher might offer me for that book, and others in the deal, make more sense up–front than smaller sales over many decades? Does the offer equal what I might earn from that book over the rest of my life, because I own all the rights to it? Can the publisher make an offer that makes business sense to both them and me, so that we both feel we're getting a fair slice of the cake? Are they going to offer better rights–reversion clauses? Or will they try to hinder my independent publishing with clauses that now often appear in publishing contracts, designed to stem the flow of authors going independent?

These are the questions I would ask now if such a deal was in the offing. But I would never rule out entirely working with a publisher again, because being a hybrid author offers the very best of both worlds. To me, the very best of *both* worlds is what an author should seek; happily agented, signed to a traditional contract, with Indie titles providing income in between the bigger signings. Follow your instincts and your agent's advice if you have one, and always remember to look after Number One.

"Neither traditional nor independent publishing is safe and neither is predictable. This year, for the first time ever, I will make more money from independent publishing than traditional. Next year, who knows? But at least with independent publishing you have some control and you know your next book actually will be published, since you are publishing it. It is also easier to make some money from your backlist, which helps smooth a career in lean years. Best to keep your options open and do both if you can."

Michael Ridpath bestselling 'hybrid' thriller author

XVIII: Getting the last word in: a summary.

1) USE A *SINGLE* NAME.

Forget the crap about *nom de plumes*. You want a brand with your name, or your chosen author name, writ *large* upon it that is highly consistent. Anything else means you have to start over to gain a new audience for another name. (Ignore this only if you normally write cozy mystery but are now considering embarking on a novel about sado–masochistic vampire ninja dwarfs. In that case you probably *need* the brand distinction to avoid terrorising your existing readers).

2) START A MAILING LIST. *NOW!*

Build it. Spend money to build it. Nourish it and cherish it and use it, because if you've got enough of them those super–fans can take you to the top without a penny spent on advertising.

3) HAVE A PLAN.

Think about your genre and target for maximum readership. You may like writing about a gentlemanly croquet dispute in pre–war India, but don't expect to earn much when it's published to no fanfare whatsoever.

4) WRITE SERIES TITLES IF YOU WANT TO SELL.

Series books always outsell stand–alone titles.

5) DON'T SPEND A FORTUNE.

Learn to design your own covers, to create your own HTML version of your book for Kindle, to edit well and to seek out new means of improving your brand. I learned all the above through *effort*, nothing more than that. It's saved me countless thousands of dollars and means that every inch of my books are my own. About the only thing I do outsourcing for is the audiobooks, because that's a real skill that I don't possess. If money's tight, apply *effort* to achieve your goals.

6) GIVE READERS A REASON TO LOVE YOU.

Not just for your work, but for the way you treat them. When I launch a new title, I launch it at $0.99 / £0.99 for a week or so and inform my mailing list and all followers so that they can buy the book at a bargain price. (I mail them in equal numbers over ten days, splitting my list accordingly, to keep sustained high sales and thus "tickle" Amazon's algorithms along with paid advertising – this avoids a sales "spike" and Amazon pulling the ranking back down too soon, which its algorithms are also programmed to do if a sales spike is too high). My promise to all of my fans is that they'll never have to pay full price for one of my books again, and I keep that promise. Their massed purchases push my books up the charts during the launch, their reviews give the book high star–ratings, and then I raise the price to full which generates a sense of quality about my books to the wider audience that follows, negating the idea in some reader's minds that a cheap book must somehow logically be "crap".

7) GET ARC AND PROOF READERS.

If you have a mailing list, they're already in there somewhere. My books are proof–read now by a dozen "super–fans" who pick up on everything that I've missed in return for a free preview copy of the book before its official publication. ARC readers also get a free book and post reviews to Amazon in return (and they always state that they got the book for free in return for an honest review, which is generally okay by Amazon, although they seem to change their rules as often as the wind. Check often to see what Amazon's current thinking is on this matter).

8) *BELIEEEEEVE* IN YOURSELF.

The only thing between you and a living as a writer nowadays is yourself, because without the absolute need for agents and publishers you are connecting directly with readers via their (and your) chosen vendors. Modest sales can equate to terrific income as an Indie. Your goal really *is* within your reach,

9) IF YOU WANT FULL TIME RESULTS, YOU NEED FULL TIME EFFORT.

By definition, as an aspiring author you may not be able to work full time at writing yet, but if you're determined to succeed you should do as much as is reasonably possible to pursue your goal. I worked 60 hour weeks at my Indie writing from 2014 onward, more than I ever did for a traditional publisher. I worked in the evenings, at weekends, when I didn't want to, when I was feeling ill, when our daughter was an infant and awake at all hours of the night, when I was tired, wired, demotivated, unsure of myself or just plain sick of writing. Sit down. Turn the computer on. Write. No excuses.

10) LIVE.

Despite all the above, learn not to obsess. Be measured in your mind before you go mental at the keyboard. Want it, believe in it and your ability to achieve it, but don't kick the husband or wife out if they dare speak at the wrong time and spoil your muse. Learn to *love* writing, to be excited by a new idea rather than just bracing yourself for the effort of writing it, and the rest will come on its own. Ultimately, our health and our happiness outweigh any bank balance. I have made myself a successful author through hard graft and not turned into a dribbling maniac with one madly twitching eye, but I've always been driven to succeed and been able to cope with high workloads. Success can come gently as well as quickly. Enjoy the ride rather than making yourself want to get off again.

Ultimately, for an author with a modicum of talent, a living as a writer is well within anybody's reach, more so now than at any point in history thanks to independent publishing. It all boils down to how much you really, *really* want it, and that will always remain with you and you alone. Make a decision soon, develop your plot, make your plan and go for it, because if I can do it, so can you. I'll leave you once again with my own favourite catchphrase. Read it often if things get hard, because as you've seen throughout this book they often did for me too...

"I didn't get through because I was the best. I got through because I learned never to quit."
Dean Crawford, 2016

Links and further reading.

If you would like a lovely *free* novel by none other than *little–old–me*, and also a chance to see how a mailing list sign–up process works from an author's website, then please visit my website below;

www.deancrawfordbooks.com

Or search the Internet for *Instafreebie* and find The Nemesis Origin to download it for free and see how that process works;

Luigi Bonomi, my literary agent's website;
LBA Books

Contributing authors;
Joanna Penn, bestselling Indie author and entrepreneur
Michael Ridpath, bestselling *hybrid* author of financial and noir thrillers
Celina Grace, bestselling Indie author of the Kate Redman thrillers
David Gledhill, former RAF fast–jet officer–aircrew and *Indie* military thriller author
James Becker, Peter Stuart Smith, Max Adams, James Barrington, Tom Kasey, Peter Lee, Thomas Payne and Jack Steel: Bestselling, multi–genre thriller author

Official organisations;
The Society of Authors
UK Literary Agents Association
USA Literary Agents Association

Software and tutorials for independent books;
Guido Henkel "Take pride in your e-book formatting"
Notepad: HTML capable word processing software
Calibre: HTML file to e–reader format converter
Gimp: Freeware art and design package

Digital Advertising sites (subscription–based) that I have used with confidence;
BookBub - the most expensive but best advertiser
Bargain Booksy
EReader News Today
Kindle Nation Daily
AwesomeGang
BKnights, Fiverr

Mailing list traffic sites (for easy, cost–effective mailing list building);
Instafreebie
BookFunnel
Mailchimp

On–line Courses;
Self Publishing Formula; Facebook, YouTube and Twitter advertising course

ABOUT THE AUTHOR

Dean Crawford is the author of over twenty novels, including the internationally published series of thrillers featuring *Ethan Warner*, a former United States Marine now employed by a government agency tasked with investigating unusual scientific phenomena. The novels have been *Sunday Times* paperback best-sellers and have gained the interest of major Hollywood production studios. He is also the enthusiastic author of many independently published novels.

10447449R00090

Printed in Great Britain
by Amazon